Illustrating the Sermon

Thomason
11-26-91

Books in the Craft of Preaching Series

THE CRAFT OF PREACHING SERIES

Illustrating the Sermon

MICHAEL J. HOSTETLER

Ministry Resources Library

Zondervan Publishing House • Grand Rapids, MI

ILLUSTRATING THE SERMON
Copyright © 1989 by Michael J. Hostetler

MINISTRY RESOURCES LIBRARY is an imprint of
Zondervan Publishing House,
1415 Lake Drive, S.E., Grand Rapids, Michigan 49506.

Library of Congress Cataloging-in-Publication Data

Hostetler, Michael J.
   Illustrating the sermon / Michael J. Hostetler.
      p.   cm. — (The Craft of preaching series)
   "Ministry resources library."
   Bibliography: p.
   ISBN 0-310-30711-2
   1. Homiletical illustrations—History and criticism. 2. Preaching.
I. Title. II. Series.
BV4226.H6   1989   89-5635
251'.08—dc19   CIP

Edited by Martha Manikas-Foster
Designed by Louise Bauer

Printed in the United States of America

89 90 91 92 93 94 / CH / 10 9 8 7 6 5 4 3 2 1

Contents

Introduction

A popular speaker in our denomination has a knack for quoting Peanuts comic strip stories. He uses them successfully to introduce and illustrate his sermons. Not long after attending a conference where this speaker gave the keynote address, my young assistant was scheduled to preach on a Sunday evening. Sure enough, he started out with a Peanuts quote and worked several more into his message. The effect? Hardly any. Although for one preacher good old Charlie Brown was compellingly alive, for the other he was dead on arrival.

This story does more than illustrate the futility of imitating another speaker's materials or techniques. It raises important questions about the matter of illustrating the biblical sermon. What makes for a good illustration? Why does an illustration work well for one speaker and flop for another? Can a speaker know ahead of time whether an illustration will be moving and interesting? What kinds of illustrations impress a modern audience? Are they the same as those that worked on audiences in the 19th and early 20th centuries? Where do good illustrations come from? Are books or floppy disks of compiled illustrations worthwhile as resources? The list of questions could go on.

Sermons need illustrations. Anyone who would argue the point has lost his homiletical marbles. Every parish preacher needs illustrations for the upcoming sermon, but not every preacher finds what he or she is looking for. Others, however, seem to have uncanny success in coming up with just the right material. Is this skill inborn or can it be learned? I believe that it can be learned, and that is the basic premise of this book.

ILLUSTRATING THE SERMON

A generation ago, William Sangster wrote, "Educating one's intuition for the sound illustration is a primary task."[1] The purpose of this book is to help practicing preachers and students of preaching sharpen the intuitive skills necessary for illustrating their sermons. Here are several points about this intuitive ability.

First, intuition for what works in communication is no substitute for exposition of the Word of God. Witty puns and interesting stories may keep a church entertained, but only the solid teaching of the Bible will keep it fed. Our communicative talents, no matter how well developed, must be made subservient to Scripture.

Second, intuition is not all serendipity. It needs to be grounded in reflection, analysis, and knowledge. Experienced as well as beginning preachers need to review the basic principles of sound preaching and illustrating.

Third, a preacher's intuitive communication skills must not be allowed to remain static. What worked when Sangster wrote about illustrations may not work today. In our age of rapidly changing mass culture, a preacher's perspective must change often to stay on the cutting edge of the congregation's needs and concerns.

Fourth, "educating one's intuition for the sound illustration" involves time, quality, and quantity. When it comes to time, most pastors feel like Sunday arrives every third or fourth day. Time constraints are a perpetual ministry challenge. Therefore, the more quickly you can find an illustration, the better. Speed, however, must be accompanied by quality. You want the best illustration you can find, not just the one you can find the fastest. In terms of quantity, the number of illustrations you use is important. Very few sermons are over-illustrated; multitudes are under-illustrated. As you sharpen your intuitive skills in illustrating, you should find more quality illustrations more quickly.

This book is not intended to be an exhaustive, theoretical treatment of sermon illustrations. At the outset of his book on the subject, Ian MacPherson said he had consulted over 300 books on preaching.[2] The scope of the present volume is far more modest. My goal has been not to write everything there is to know about sermon illustrations, but to write of the more important things a pastor needs to know to become a more effective communicator of God's Word.

Acknowledgments

The author is grateful for permission to use extensive quotations from the following works:

"The Baptist on the Bridge" routine was transcribed from video. It has been produced by Epic Records on the LP album $E=MO^2$ and in the HBO Home Video Series "Emo Philips Live From the Hasty Pudding Theatre." Used by permission of the artist.

Out of the Saltshaker and Into the World by Rebecca Manley Pippert. Copyright © 1979 by InterVarsity Christian Fellowship of the USA and used by permission of InterVarsity Press, P.O. Box 1400, Downers Grove, IL 60515.

Out of Africa by Isak Dinesen. Copyright © 1937 by Random House, Inc., and renewed 1965 by Rungsted-lundfonden. Reprinted by permission of the publisher.

1

Definitions

Modern preachers of every tradition have acknowledged the crucial importance of illustrations in preaching. Few would argue with George Sweazey who offers eleven reasons why illustrations are "indispensable."[1] While it is outside the scope of some preaching texts to deal specifically with illustrations,[2] most deal with the subject to some degree. Book-length treatments of illustrating include Sangster's oft reprinted *The Craft of Sermon Illustration* (W. L. Jenkins, 1950), and Ian MacPherson's *Art of Illustrating Sermons* (originally published by Abingdon Press, reissued by Baker Book House).

An exception to the general enthusiasm for illustrations is Fred B. Craddock who declares, " . . . a sermon may not need illustrations."[3] However, Craddock does emphasize that the most important illustrative forms are clear style and extended anecdotes or stories.[4]

While there is widespread agreement on the importance of illustrations, it is difficult to find consensus on a definition. Some writers, like MacPherson, have despaired of finding a comprehensive definition. Citing Shakespeare's character, Bardolf, who defined "accommodating," as "that is, when a man is, as they say, accommodated; or when a man is, being, whereby a' may be thought to be accommodated," MacPherson believes "the best line is to try to define [illustrations] according to function."[5]

Other authors have looked to etymology for help in defining illustrations. The word "illustrate" derives from the Latin verb, *illustrare*, meaning to light up or illuminate. One of the most memorable similes in homiletical literature is Charles Haddon Spurgeon's comparison of illustrations to windows: "Illustrations, like windows, let light into the mind."[6] One modern writer takes issue with Spurgeon, saying illustrations are more like doors than windows.[7] Spurgeon would not object. Spurgeon also called illustrations fish hooks because "illustrations stick in the soul like hooks in a fish's mouth."[8]

Even though difficult, defining the illustration is important. Most preachers need to get a firmer grasp on what a sermon illustration is, or, taking the cue from MacPherson, what it does, theoretically and practically. An analysis of the concept, especially in its verbal form, "to illustrate," lays the foundation for "educating one's intuition for the sound illustration."

Theoretically, we could define illustrating as making a verbal foray from the realm of the abstract to the realm of the particular. "Abstract" simply refers to something that is thought of apart from any particular instances or material objects. Preaching deals with abstractions. Haddon Robinson writes, "Skilled preachers deal in high and low levels of abstraction, climbing back and forth like a laborer on a ladder. To have meaning, particulars must be gathered up in generalizations, and abstractions must be taken down to particulars to be made understandable."[9]

Illustrating is an attempt to move verbally from the top of the ladder, the realm of abstraction, down to the level of the particular and familiar. Depravity, for example, is a theological abstraction at the top of the ladder. Depravity doesn't illustrate sins; sins illustrate depravity. The goal of illustrating is to move the theological abstraction down to a familiar level. This is not to say that in sermon delivery you will never go the other way, from the particular to the abstract. On the contrary, all illustrations appear to do that. But the ultimate reason they go up the ladder is to bring something down.

Making the abstract particular is essentially what the Bible is all about. "God" is the greatest abstraction of all. Everything about God is abstract: the Trinity, holiness, wrath, goodness, love, forgiveness, incarnation, and so on. As God's revelation of himself to the human race, the Bible is one huge illustration. Its law, history, prophecy, poetry, and letters make particular the truths about God he has chosen to reveal.

Just because the Bible is the greatest illustration of all, however, does not mean it is easy to read or preach. J. I. Packer sums up our dilemma in approaching the Bible as follows:

> Our Bible-reading takes us into what, for us, is quite a new world—namely, the near Eastern world as it was thousands of years ago, primitive and barbaric, agricultural and unmechanized. It is in that world that the action of the Bible story is played out. In that world we meet Abraham, and Moses, and David, and the rest, and watch God dealing with them. We hear the prophets denouncing idolatry and threatening judgment upon sin. We see the Man of Galilee, doing miracles, arguing with the Jews, dying for sinners, rising from death and ascending to heaven. We read letters from Christian teachers directed against strange errors which as far as we know, do not now exist. It is all intensely interesting, but it all seems very far away.[10]

At least three specific factors tend to create the distance that we find between the abstractions of religious truth and the commonplaces of daily living. The distancing factors are language, history, and conception. Language is a factor because the Bible was written in Hebrew, Aramaic, and Greek, which are vastly different conceptually from modern English. A linguistic-cultural distance exists that even the best translation cannot completely cross. Creating historical distance is the fact that most recent biblical writings are nearly 2,000 years old. Time has created a chasm between the biblical world and our own. Finally, on the conceptual level, theological ideas like "holiness" or "joy" are distant from our normal interaction with things and events.

What follows are three sermon illustrations which themselves illustrate how a preacher can cross the linguistic, historical, and conceptual chasms between abstract and familiar.

An example of linguistic distance is the biblical expression, "the hand of God," which appears over 200 times in the Old Testament alone. The following illustration helps evoke a little of what the phrase means.

> When George VI gave his Christmas address to the British people in 1939, the Second World War had just begun. The German armies had conquered Northern Europe and the long night of war lay ahead. In his speech the King quoted these words from a book by M. Louise Haskins, "And I said to the man who stood at the gate of the year: 'Give me a light that I may tread safely into the unknown.' And he replied: 'Go out into the darkness and put your hand into the hand of God. That shall be to you better than light and safer than a known way.' "

Time also creates abstraction. What happened long ago strikes us as remote and not a little irrelevant. The next illustration was used by the American preacher, Harry Ironside, to explain a historical occurrence: the multiple authorship and long term compilation of the Psalter.

> We call this book ordinarily, "The Psalms of David," but David did not write them all. A great many of them were written by other people. They were the Psalms of David in the sense that we call the old gospel hymn book, "The Moody and Sankey Hymn Book." Moody did not write any of the hymns and Sankey only a sprinkling of them, but these men compiled the book. If you go over to Great Britain today you can go to the

original publishers of it and say "I would like to have a copy of the Moody and Sankey Hymn Book," and they will hand you a book with twelve hundred hymns in it. In the old days this book had only six hundred hymns. It was compiled by them originally, but a great many others have been added from time to time, and today there is this vast collection. We can think of the book of the Psalms of David in the same way.[11]

Ironside's analogy, although now dated, served well to make understandable the historical abstractions of multiple authorship and long-term compilation.

Abstract concepts, perhaps even more than foreign words or hoary events, need to be illustrated. Take for example the concept of "acceptance" vis-à-vis Romans 15:7: "Accept one another, then, just as Christ accepted you, in order to bring praise to God." Rebecca Manley Pippert uses the following compelling illustration.

When I first came to Portland, Oregon, I met a student on one of the campuses where I worked. He was brilliant and looked like he was always pondering the esoteric: his hair was always mussy, and in the entire time I knew him, I never once saw him wear a pair of shoes. Rain, sleet, or snow, Bill was always barefoot. While he was attending college he had become a Christian. At this time a well-dressed, middle-class church across the street from the campus wanted to develop more of a ministry to the students. They were not sure how to go about it, but they tried to make them feel welcome. One day Bill decided to worship there. He walked into this church wearing his blue jeans, tee shirt and of course no shoes. People looked a bit uncomfortable, but no one said anything. So Bill began walking down the aisle looking for a seat. The church was quite crowded that Sunday, so as he got down to the front pew and realized that there were no seats, he just squatted on the carpet—perfectly acceptable behavior at a college fellowship, but perhaps unnerving for a church congregation. The tension in the air became so thick one could slice it.

Suddenly an elderly man began walking down the aisle toward the boy. Was he going to scold Bill? My friends who saw him approaching said they thought, "You can't blame him. He'd never guess Bill is a Christian. And his world is too distant from Bill's to understand. You can't blame him for what he's going to do."

As the man kept walking slowly down the aisle, the church became utterly silent, all eyes were focused on him, you could not hear anyone breathe. When the man reached Bill, with some difficulty he lowered himself and sat down next to him on the carpet. He and Bill worshiped together on the floor that Sunday. I was told there was not a dry eye in the congregation.[12]

Illustrating is making a verbal foray from the realm of the abstract to the realm of the particular. If this definition is a bit too theoretical, try this one: illustrating is speaking words in a sermon which substantiate, amplify, explain, or add emotional proof to the points of the sermon.

The more practical definition complements the theoretical. Conceptually, we need to understand what we, as preachers, are ultimately about—making the abstract particular. In the study and pulpit, however, we need to know what we are actually doing—trying to make a point from the Bible. It's one thing to understand the principles of marine biology and another to pull a bass out of a weedy pond. The rest of this book is about how to fill your creel.

On the practical level, the three illustrations above accomplish one or more of the tasks mentioned in the second, practical, definition. The story about King George is good for its emotive appeal. Using the Haskins' quote without mention of the King's use of it in 1939, would not have the same appeal. The illustration gives the "hand of God" expression the dramatic importance it deserves.

Harry Ironside's illustration is a simple explanatory analogy. It also, however, substantiates the historical fact of the Psalter's compilation by showing that the very same sort of thing happens to hymn books today. The Pippert story has emotive power while at the same time amplifying the biblical concepts of acceptance and love.

Illustrating might be likened to footlights, doors, windows, fish hooks, or simply certain kinds of "words in a sermon." Take your pick. It is not important what you call it, but that you do it. Having considered what it is to illustrate, we are ready to take a look at the kinds of materials that can be used as illustrations.

2

Types

Ralph Waldo Emerson once remarked, "I cannot hear a sermon without being struck by the fact that amid drowsy series of sentences what a sensation a historical fact, a biographical name, a sharply objective illustration makes! Why will not the preacher heed the admonition of the momentary silence of his congregation (and often what is shown him) that this particular sentence is all they carry away?"[1]

Like many others, Emerson saw the value of illustrations amidst the somnolent statements of biblical discourse. The question that confronts sermon-makers is, What types of material make the best illustrations? Emerson mentions history and biography. What else is there?

The noun "illustration" itself is too vague to describe anything particular. We will regard it as a comprehensive term referring to any and all verbal forays from the realm of the abstract to the particular. Under this comprehensive definition of illustration, four particular forms are most important: anecdotes, quotations, statistics, and live demonstrations. Every preacher's intuition should be trained to find and use these kinds of illustrations.

ANECDOTES

The attitude of homileticians toward the anecdote has changed considerably over the years. Traditionally, the anecdote has been criticized and belittled. Even Sangster, writing as late as 1950, had serious reservations about the appropriateness of anecdotes in a sermon.[2] Just one generation later, however, John Stott, writing in 1982, claims, "The most effective illustrations, however, are probably anecdotes . . ."[3]

The discomfort of previous generations of preachers with the anecdote derives from the usage of the word itself. According to *Webster's Twentieth Century Dictionary*, anecdotes originally were "little-known, entertaining facts of history or biography." At one time, *anecdote* seems to have carried the connotation of triviality on the level of the trivia of "Trivial Pursuit." More recently, however, *anecdote* has lost this connotation (we now use the word *trivia*), and simply refers to "a short, entertaining account of some happening, usually personal or biographical." No preacher today needs to apologize for using an anecdote. All preachers should be familiar with the following five types of anecdotes.

Biblical Anecdotes

Using the stories of the Bible to illustrate points in the sermon is a double-edged sword. On the one hand, citing the Bible serves the purpose of promoting Christian education by calling to mind biblical episodes. On the other hand, biblical anecdotes tend to reveal biblical illiteracy. There's a good chance no one in the audience will know what you are talking about. For example, the Nazarites provide a wonderful Old Testament example of commitment to piety. But who in your audience has heard of them?

Never underestimate biblical ignorance even in churches with comprehensive educational programs and highly biblicist theologies. Only very familiar Bible stories

20

(Adam and Eve, Noah and the Ark, David and Bathsheba, and the like) can be used as illustrations without accompanying explanations. And remember, good illustrations don't need explaining. It may be that the Bible should be used more for poignant quotations than familiar anecdotes (as discussed below).

Historical Anecdotes

History offers a rich store of provocative and memorable illustrations. (I define a historical anecdote as an incident predating the speaker's lifetime.) The further back you go, the less useful the anecdote. When using a historical illustration, make sure to include a good number of details (dates, names, places), and be certain that all of your information is accurate. Historical anecdotes may run the gamut from ancient to modern times, but keep in mind that the less familiar the epoch, the more difficult it will be for the audience to stay with you.

The late Dr. Harold J. Ockenga used the following historical allusion in a published sermon on Christ's second coming:

> At this time believers will be exhibited as the sons of God, the heirs of the kingdom, and the rulers of the world. When Octavian was sixteen years of age he was designated by Julius Caesar as his successor. At nineteen he was in command of an army and was away from Rome. At the hands of Brutus, Cassius, and other friends, Julius Caesar was assassinated. Octavian had not received the public adoption by Julius as his son and heir. Therefore, he had to fight his way to the sovereignty of the empire. The old Roman practice of public adoption of one to become a successor and heir illustrates what will some day take place for the sons of God. They will be publicly declared God's heirs . . . [4]

This illustration is pertinent to the text (2 Thessalonians 1:10), but it exudes a certain mustiness. Few modern listeners are the least familiar with classical antiquity. Of greater power are incidents nearer us in time and interest. The following illustration relates to how Christ frees his people from the fear of death (Hebrews 2:15).

> During the second world war, Sir John Laurence attended what he describes as "a sort of Communist memorial service" to Stanislavsky in the Moscow Arts Theatre. "There was a closed coffin on the stage, draped in a red flag, and the dead man's colleagues came and said goodbye to him in set speeches. One heard some of the world's greatest actors and actresses speaking of their teacher and leader on what should have been a moving occasion, but the experience was empty. I was not at that time a Christian believer, but even so it struck me that Communism has nothing to say about death. There was no development of a theme such as one gets in the prayer book service for the Burial of the Dead. In the same way to visit the mausoleum where Lenin lies . . . is for me a disturbing experience precisely because it has no content."[5]

This illustration carries emotive appeal even though it needs more specific identification of John Laurence and Stanislavsky.

Personal Anecdotes

Personal anecdotes are those that involve the firsthand experience of the speaker. Don't underestimate the value of your own observations and experiences. The preacher's educational experiences, travels, family life, and pastoral work are excellent illustration sources.[6]

Guiding the use of personal anecdotes are honest humility and professional integrity. Both self-deprecation and self-aggrandizement must be avoided. Refreshing honesty in the pulpit will foster open sharing in the whole church. On the other hand, standards of confidentiality require some anecdotes to remain untold. If you have even the slightest doubt about the appropriateness of going public with an anecdote, don't do it. Changing names and details of a true story in order to make it usable in a sermon constitutes double fraud: breach of confidentiality plus fabrication. Use personal anecdotes that pass the twin tests of honesty and integrity.

One of my own memorable experiences has served well as an illustration of the biblical concept of lostness and similar ideas:

> Shortly after moving to New York, I took my children to the Macy's Thanksgiving Day Parade. Times Square was a crush of humanity, but we managed to find a decent vantage point for the parade. As the floats and balloons started to pass us, everyone squeezed forward for a better view. I was keeping track of where each of our three boys stood, but suddenly I realized I could no longer see my six-year-old. I had a sick feeling that something terrible was happening. For ten panic-filled minutes that seemed like hours, I moved up and down the parade line looking and shouting his name. Finally I spotted him sitting serenely on the pavement with some other kids enthralled by the passing spectacle. My joy of finding him quickly gave way to the anger of having lost him in the first place and was followed by the sense of relief that the ordeal was over.

Contemporary Anecdotes

Contemporary anecdotes are recent events (within the speaker's lifetime) that do not involve the speaker. Most anecdotes probably fall into this category. They are current events, the stuff of the news and public discourse. Contemporary anecdotes are culled from the pages of newspapers and magazines as well as from the electronic media. Topics may range from aardvarks to zygotes. The preacher's own creative imagination sees the connection between the anecdote and the sermon point.

While preparing a sermon on Psalm 19, ("The heavens declare the glory of God . . . "), I came across an article about a recent breakthrough in astronomy. Here's how I made the connection between the two.

> On a rock-strewn plateau above the treeline in the foothills of the French Alps, a French astronomer named Antoine Labeyrie is revolutionizing the technology of making telescopes. Using a technique called optical interferometry, he is constructing a telescope that will give scientists a sharper image of distant stars than they have ever had. Instead of seeing stars as mere points of light, the new instrument will show them as actual disks. As I recently read about his new advance in astronomy, it struck me that for all our technological sophistication, twentieth century people are as fascinated with the night sky as any of our ancestors. We are separated from the great affirmations about the glorious heavens in the Psalms by time, but not by interest.

Fictional Anecdotes

Fictional anecdotes are drawn from the world of fiction in literature, film, and television, including special forms such as fables, allegories, parables, and myths. (Contemporary audiences will be far more familiar with television shows and characters than any other form of fiction.) The problem with television fiction, however, is that it is not meant for discussion or reflection. Vapid, escapist entertainment leaves little to talk about.

Most fictional anecdotes, aside from TV, require some brief explanation of plot or introduction of characters or author. For example, a particularly poignant scene from the film *Out of Africa* illustrates the value of marriage vis-à-vis Hebrews 13:4. In the movie, Meryl Streep plays opposite Robert Redford as the Danish baroness Karen Blixen. They are in love. She wants to get married; he wants his freedom to remain a playboy. In one scene they quarrel over the future as he disparages what he believes are the strictures of marriage. Finally, she can say no more than this: "There are some things in life that are so valuable that no price is too high to pay for them." Married love, of course, is one of those precious commodities.

Stories and Storytelling

Stories are related to anecdotes, but are different in both length and function. A story is longer than an anecdote. It includes a beginning, an ending, and plot in between) The story is also more self-contained than the anecdote. The anecdote generally points beyond itself to a biblical or sermonic abstraction which it is intended to particularize. The story, on the other hand, points to itself. It embodies the idea to be communicated.

Recently many have held up the story as the best of all sermon forms.[7] It is in this train of thought that Fred Craddock disparages what are commonly regarded as "illustrations." He writes "Actually, in good preaching what is referred to as illustrations are, in fact, stories or anecdotes which do not illustrate the point; rather they *are* the point. In other words, a story may carry in its bosom the whole message rather than the illumination of a message which had already been related in another but less clear way."[8]

Is the story the ultimate sermonic form and premier mode of illustration? Is a preacher really a storyteller? Sweazey states flatly, "The art of storytelling has no place in the pulpit beyond where it serves the sermon's purpose."[9] For practical reasons, he insists that anecdotes be brief.

Theological considerations, however, also come to bear on the idea of the sermon as story. Evangelical preachers will insist—to borrow Craddock's phrase—that the message has indeed "already been related in another but less clear way." The Bible, not the story, is the Word of God. The Story has already been told. In this sense all illustrations, including stories, mediate rather than embody the message. Evangelicals will not feel comfortable with Craddock's approach because it blurs the distinction between text and sermon, the Word of God and the word of the preacher.

In spite of its theological shortcomings, however, the

sermon-as-story approach offers practical insights into effective illustrating. First, it warns us away from what Charles Rice calls "the 'professional' anecdote, the canned story which is not really owned by the preacher and the congregation."[10] And, second, it emphasizes the importance of the delivery of anecdotes which touches on the art of narration or storytelling. Nothing wrecks great material more efficiently than poor delivery. Most preachers, lacking adequate training in seminary, would do well to read up on storytelling or, even better, take a class in narration at a college or university.[11]

QUOTATIONS

The second major type of illustration is the quotation. Anecdotes and statistics can be quoted in the sermon, but the quotation itself is defined as a relevant statement of authority. Good quotations have both qualities: relevance and authority. Relevance has to do with what is said. Its connection to the point at hand must be clear. For example, a saying of Søren Kierkegaard, "Life must be lived forwards, but can only be understood backwards," might be apropos to a sermon on the lessons of biblical history, but would hardly be relevant to a sermon on prophecy.

A quotation's authority hinges on who said it. Especially when making a controversial point, an authoritative quotation bolsters the argument. Audience analysis is important at this point. Not all authorities and audiences connect. Study your audience before quoting Dietrich Bonhoeffer, Martin Luther King, Jr., or Bob Jones, Sr. Biblical quotations are good because of the Bible's unparalleled authority.

What should a preacher look for in a quotation, in addition to relevance and authority?

Brevity

Long quotations are deadly. The shorter the better. Often phrases or sentences can be edited out of a long quotation, making it more manageable without affecting its content. A classic biblical example is the discussion of husbands and wives in Ephesians 5:25–33. Paul makes a major digression in the passage to discuss the relationship of Christ and the Church. Verses 26, 27, and 33 can easily be edited from the quotation if the preacher's emphasis is on marriage. (Editing serves both to shorten and focus the quotation.)

Aphorisms

An aphorism is a short, concise statement of a principle or maxim.) Aphorisms are more interesting than ordinary declarative sentences. My assistant once said in a sermon, "God is not calling us to believe in total surrender; he's calling us to total surrender." The following sentence says the same thing but is not quotable. "God is calling us to go beyond believing in total surrender as an idea, to practicing it as a way of life." What's the difference? Word choice, conciseness, and the juxtaposition of concepts contribute to quotable material. (Printed collections of quotations are valuable if they contain many aphorisms.)

Attention and Application

Since a sermon is not an academic thesis, do not use quotations to explain the text. Explain the Bible in your own words. (Unless you have adopted a controversial interpretation that needs an authoritative back-up.) Use quotations to capture the audience's attention or to drive home a point of application.)

Simplicity

The more you need to say about a quotation, the less valuable it is. (No word in the quotation should need to be defined for the audience.) Some quotations that work in print might not be successful in spoken discourse. Sir William

Osler once said, "Superfluity of lecturing causes ischial bursitis." An educated reader will probably recognize *ischial* as an anatomical term. A listener, however, is much more likely to miss the word altogether.

The source of the quotation should need no introduction ("Abraham Lincoln once said . . . ") or only a very brief one ("Epictetus, a Stoic philosopher of New Testament times, said . . . "). If the quotation is anonymous, a simple "It has been said . . . " will do. Obviously, a quotation without the authority that comes with authorship will need to be highly relevant.

Some pitfalls to avoid in using quotations are long poems, muddled attribution, and bracketing.

Poems

Two or three lines of pertinent verse are acceptable in a sermon, but usually no more. Modern audiences are not disposed to listening to poetry any more than preachers are trained for reading it. Hymns are the exceptions. Because of their simplicity, familiarity, and devotional value, hymns can be quoted freely, but such quotations should be limited to one or two verses.

Muddled Attribution

Do not attribute to a novelist or playwright lines spoken by characters in novels or plays. Poor William Shakespeare has been cited for every utterance of Falstaff, Iago, and Juliet.

Bracketing

Do not bracket the quotation with the trite phrases: "And I quote" or "End quote." Also avoid the habit of wiggling two fingers of each hand to indicate a quotation. Introduce a quotation by simply mentioning the source. When reading a quotation, voice pitch and volume should rise slightly and rate of speech should diminish. A brief pause at the end indicates to the audience that the quotation is finished.

Finally, two questions govern all quotations. First, can I say this better myself? If the answer is no, then quote. Second, do I need this added authority for the point I want to make? If the answer is yes, then quote. Don't be embarrassed to quote. Quoting is a first-rate rhetorical technique to enhance attention and strengthen arguments.

STATISTICS

Statistics are an integral part of the Age of Information. Computers can turn out statistics faster than the collective mind of humanity can absorb them. The news media as well as the government have fallen in love with statistics. As a result, statistics are a part of all public discourse—including preaching. Statistics commonly heard in the pulpit relate to church growth, divorce rates, stewardship issues, and the overall state of religion. The Church Growth Movement and the Gallup Organization turn out a great number of statistics about religion.

Several guidelines regarding statistics must be kept in mind. First, realize that many statistics are abstract. For example, the age of the earth, expressed in billions of years, is a hopeless abstraction. A science writer once offered this comparison:

> If the earth's history could be compressed into a single year, the first eight months would be completely without life, the next two would see only the primitive creatures, mammals wouldn't appear until the second week in December, and no *homo sapiens* until 11:45 PM on Dec. 31. The entire period of man's written history would occupy the final 60 seconds before midnight.[12]

Just because many statistics are abstract does not mean they should be avoided. Choose the most understandable statistics and particularize them as needed (such as rounding off large numbers or breaking down totals per capita).

Another guideline for using statistics is not to overuse them. Consider the following section from a church management book.

> The result was that by the early 1980's, 16 percent of all Americans born before 1924 identified themselves as Methodists, but only 7.7 percent of those born in the 1958–65 era called themselves Methodists. Likewise slightly over 6 percent of the population born before 1924 are Presbyterians compared to only 3 percent born in the 1958–65 period. The figures are not quite as dismal for Lutherans, but the trend is the same. While 9.5 percent of those born before 1924 claim to be Lutherans, only 5.7 percent of those born during the 1958–65 era call themselves Lutherans. A similar pattern prevails for Episcopalians as slightly over 3 percent born in the first quarter of this century identify themselves as Episcopalians compared to 1.8 percent for those born during 1958–65.
>
> By contrast, 13 percent of those born before 1924, 13 percent of those born during 1924–57, and 14 percent of those born in the 1958–65 era identify themselves as Southern Baptists.[13]

Statistic babble like this is almost unreadable, but in spoken discourse it is worse. When used in print, and especially if used in a speech, large quantities of statistics must be packaged in charts and graphs.

A third guideline in using statistics is to be as accurate as possible. Do your research before you post the numbers. Is the average you are citing a median average or an arithmetic average? Have the numbers you are using to show a trend been researched over a long enough period to prove a trend? Are you sure, for instance, that ten percent of your church members give ninety percent of the offerings?

Finally, be advised that statistics, especially surprising ones, will be met with scepticism. The old saying is that figures don't lie, but liars figure. Everyone thinks that statistics can be used to prove anything and a few folks agree with Benjamin Disraeli who said, "There are three kinds of lies: lies, damned lies, and statistics."

LIVE DEMONSTRATIONS

Occasionally some sort of demonstration that illustrates a sermon point will come to mind. Many years ago I witnessed a fine example of a live demonstration of 2 Peter 1:5–7. In the text, Peter explains how Christians are to progressively add to rudimentary faith the qualities of goodness, knowledge, self-control, perseverance, godliness, brotherly kindness, and love. During the sermon, the preacher asked the church pianist to come to the piano and play "Jesus Loves Me." First he asked the pianist to play with one finger, then one hand, then four part harmony, and finally with full accompaniment. He then explained that the melody line was like faith, recognizable when played with one finger but made steadily stronger and more beautiful by the addition of more notes. It was a wonderful illustration that I will never forget.

Live demonstrations certainly have biblical precedent. Consider the didactic antics of Ezekiel (e.g., Ezek. 12:3–6) or even the marriage of the prophet Hosea (Hos. 1:2–3). The possibilities for live demonstrations today are limited only by a preacher's imagination. A Christmas Eve sermon was once introduced by a mock radio broadcast over the church's public address system. The "announcer" read an evocative piece originally broadcast over CBS Radio in 1939, called "Christmas in the Trenches" by William White. The "broadcast" set the tone for a sermon with the same title.

On another occasion, to illustrate the reality of state persecution of Christians, a preacher had several off-duty, uniformed police officers barge into the middle of the service and "arrest" the preacher. Some parishioners felt this illustration was a bit much.

Live demonstrations are rare because of the time and imagination it takes to prepare them. Cutting corners in preparation, however, is likely to create a flop. Enlist the help of other people and plan rehearsals. Further, be judicious in choosing the occasion for a live demonstration. A New Year's Eve service may be far more appropriate than Easter Sunday morning.

In summary, the homiletical intuition needs to be tuned in to four major types of illustrations: anecdotes, quotations, statistics, and live demonstrations. The four are not of equal importance. Anecdotes are most important, followed by quotations, and then statistics and live demonstrations. All four, however, should be familiar to the preacher who wants to communicate effectively. Another key to effective communication is style itself, which will be our next consideration.

3

Style

One of Solomon's proverbs declares: "A word aptly spoken is like apples of gold in settings of silver" (Proverbs 25:11). The aptly spoken word is the heart of effective communication style. Such beautiful words, however, are not all that easy to find in popular discourse.

In lamenting the fact that "Americans don't talk as colorfully as they used to," the noted columnist, Russell Baker, cites two reasons for the prevalence of drab language.

> One is that since the social ban on dirty talk was dropped in the late 1960's, the subsequent generation has been too busy talking dirty to cultivate the art of talking colorfully. Another is that the collapse of education aimed at civilizing people has created a population as ignorant of poetry as it is of history and geography.[1]

The pulpit has yet to be overtaken by the trend to dirty talk, but it is still a great bastion of drab talk. The golden apples in silver settings are seldom seen in church. Dullness, however, can be overcome by giving attention to style.

Style might be considered as another type of illustration, alongside anecdotes, quotations, statistics, and live demonstrations. Craddock seems to advocate style as the only type of illustration necessary.

> The fact is, if consistent attention is given to the language, very little illustrative material is needed, while the hearers will very likely give the preacher credit for using helpful illustrations. What is clear does not need to be illustrated because it seems already to be full of light.[2]

What Craddock is speaking of is style. Style is like the other types of illustrations but transcends them all, permeating the sermon altogether.

Defining style is notoriously difficult. Haddon Robinson refers to it as "choice of words."[3] Selection of words, however, is not all there is to it. Well-chosen words must be arranged creatively. Apt words must be aptly spoken.

In the definitive volume on English usage, *The Elements of Style*, William Strunk leads us to what may be the best definition of style. He refers to it as the spark that ignites a certain combination of words, causing them to explode in the mind.[4] Style depends on both content (the right combination of words) and creative power (the spark that ignites the words).

Style goes to the heart of sermon illustrating. It reflects a preacher's ability to move comfortably up and down the ladder from the abstract to the particular. Why do some preachers always seem to be at the top of the ladder, lost in clouds of abstraction, regardless of the quality or number of their illustrations? The answer may lie in two factors critical to the development of style. Style is built on both a clear understanding of, and firm belief in, what is being preached.

If a preacher does not clearly understand the abstraction to be communicated (redemption, depravity, the afterlife), then it is likely he or she will get stuck in abstractions. Style is thwarted because of confusion over the combination of words at hand. There can be no explosion if the explosives are unrecognized, lost, scattered, or misunderstood. For all the theological education preachers are subjected to, surprisingly few seem to clearly comprehend the basic ideas preaching is meant to convey.

The other hindrance to style is lack of belief. If, for example, the preacher does not really believe in the Virgin Birth, he or she will be more comfortable to dally in abstractions about it than to draw concrete conclusions from it. The right combinations of words may be in place, but without the spark to ignite them.

A preacher who understands the biblical text clearly and believes it fervently has taken the first steps toward developing effective style. Other factors, however, are also needed. To shift the metaphor, just as there are many techniques to produce a spark, many techniques contribute to style. The following four suggestions will help you become more aware of good style and how to develop it.

The first suggestion is to study the nature of style. It doesn't take long to read Strunk and White's *The Elements of Style*, or a similar volume. Most major homiletics texts include chapters on style. George Sweazey, for example, discusses style by identifying seven of its most notable qualities: simplicity, clarity, logic, interest, beauty, mood, and length.[5] Studying what style is all about will help you determine how dull you are and what you can do about it. Awareness of what constitutes style is the first step toward livelier communication.

The second suggestion for developing better style is to concentrate on figures of speech and qualities of words. Style is especially dependent upon analogies of all kinds, from simple similes to complicated metaphors. One writer described homesickness as "one of those things you can't forget if you've experienced it." "Like what?" we are prone to ask. "Like sky diving or falling in love with the best looking guy in the senior class when you are a freshman with bad skin and posture."[6] Comparisons are the stuff of style.

Word quality involves both evocative power and euphony. Specific nouns and powerful verbs usually make for good style. Why say "sound," if you really mean "euphony"? Why opt for "took" or "went" when you could use

35

"seized" and "traveled"? Choosing the most specific noun or evocative verb will take time and might require the use of thesaurus and dictionary, but the results are worth it.

Euphony has to do with how words sound and is even more important in spoken discourse than in written. An essayist once described gossip as "the normal nattering background noise of civilization."[7] The phrase actually sounds like nattering background noise! Of course the quest for euphonic style can lead to absurdity. Who hasn't heard a seven point sermon in which all the points started with letter P? Nevertheless, a little attention to the sounds of words can make for memorable style.

A third suggestion for the development of style is to read the masters of good style like Malcolm Muggeridge, Madeleine L'Engle, Frederick Buechner, or Garrison Keillor. The idea is not to imitate someone else's style, but to develop an intuition out of which your own style can grow. Judging from the oppressive dullness of most biblical commentaries, it is little wonder many sermons are dull. If all you read is arid academic prose, there's a good chance your preaching will be arid and academic.

Also in regard to reading for style, Haddon Robinson suggests reading aloud. "Reading aloud does two things for you. First, your vocabulary will increase. . . . Second, as you read style better than your own, new patterns of speech and creative wording will be etched on your nervous system. You will develop a feel for picture-making language."[8]

A fourth suggestion for developing style, which may be the most difficult, is to develop the discipline of writing out what you want to say. Nothing helps develop style as well as writing. For example, in preaching on Psalm 2, ("Why do the nations rage . . . "), I want to expand on the concept of "raging." If I use an outline, I may write down something like this:

> Raging. Defined as insanity or raving fury. Related to the word "rabies." The raging of mankind against God continues today and is as ridiculous as ever.

I have an idea of what I want to say and a few notes to guide me. Exactly how I go about expressing these ideas in the delivery of the sermon, however, is unpredictable. Whether or not my communication will ignite and explode is questionable. But if I write out exactly what I want to say, I have the opportunity to work on style—the chance to deliberately place a charge and attach a fuse.

The dictionary defines rage as insanity or raving fury. We often use it to describe natural phenomena. Interestingly, the words rage and rabies come from the same Latin root word meaning madness or raving. The effect of rabies is the same in animals and humans. As the central nervous system is destroyed, the victim falls into raving insanity.

Rage is not a delicate word, especially when it is applied to people as it is in our English versions in the first line of Psalm 2. Why do the nations rage? Why is the planet Earth in the grip of raving insanity? Why is the human race rabid? According to the second psalm, the raging sinfulness of mankind is not only violent and grotesque, but also ridiculous. The raving and plotting of sinners is comical, in a dark way, because there is a righteous God in heaven who extends his rule over the earth.

Only speakers with unusual natural ability can extemporize with vivid style. The rest of us mortals must work at it, and writing is the work. This is not to say that the sermon should be read, but that it should be written. It is important to note that writing the sermon does not necessarily cause it to lose the qualities of spoken discourse. Sweazey sensibly reminds us, "Competent authors, and certainly preachers, can write as though they were talking to someone."[9]

Great style begins as discipline and leads to artistry over a lifetime of preaching. The nineteenth century Baptist preacher, Alexander Maclaren, was one such artist. In his eulogy for Maclaren, W. Robertson Nicoll said of his style:

Maclaren resolved that he would not read sermons, but speak them, and that the spoken sermon should be as careful and polished as the written sermon. He used to say that it took him years to accomplish this, and I can well believe it, for the result was miraculous. . . . He acquired that rare faculty of speaking better English than he could write. . . . He commanded words as an emperor and as a magician. In his very loftiest flights, one hardly knew whether he spoke or sang. . . . [10]

4

Qualities

Not all illustrations are created equal. Some anecdotes and quotations have exceptional power to communicate while others fall flat. Developing a sensitive intuition for what will be effective is crucial to selecting and using illustrations. Sensing what will work, however, is not only instinctive. Investing in the stock market involves some intuition, but every stock has a price-to-earnings ratio and a yield that can be measured objectively. So it is with illustrations.

Even though selecting illustrations is sometimes simply a matter of personal taste, there are objective tests that come to bear. These objective factors can be summarized in six specific evaluative questions that should be asked of all illustrations to determine their value in the sermon.

Question One: Is It Relevant?

Every illustration, from long, quoted anecdotes to phrase-length similes, must be relevant to its point in the sermon. It doesn't matter how humorous, interesting, emotional, or up-to-date the illustration is if it doesn't connect with the point.

The following illustration, from J. B. Phillips's book *Ring of Truth*, was used to introduce an Easter sermon on the Resurrection.

> Many of us who believe in what is technically known as the Communion of Saints must have experienced the sense of nearness, for a fairly short time, of those whom we love soon after they have died. This has certainly happened to me several times. But the late C. S. Lewis, whom I did not know very well and had only seen in the flesh once, but with whom I had corresponded a fair amount, gave me an unusual experience. A few days after his death, while I was watching television, he 'appeared' sitting in a chair a few feet from me, and spoke a few words which were particularly relevant to the difficult circumstances through which I was passing. He was ruddier in complexion than ever, grinning all over his face . . . and positively glowing with health. The interesting thing to me was that I had not been thinking about him at all. I was neither alarmed nor surprised. . . . He was just *there*—"large as life and twice as natural." A week later, this time when I was in bed, reading before going to sleep, he appeared again . . . and repeated to me the same message, which was very important to me at the time. I was a little puzzled by this, and I mentioned it to a certain saintly bishop who was then living in retirement here in Dorset. His reply was, 'My dear John, this sort of thing is happening all the time.'[1]

This illustration is very powerful (perhaps too overwhelming to be of any use), but when used to illustrate the Resurrection it failed badly. Why? It's not about the Resurrection. It may say something about life after death or it may be a Protestant ghost story, but it is not all that relevant to resurrection. Every preacher must learn to ruthlessly eliminate any illustration that is not really apropos.

You must discipline yourself not to force-fit an illustration where it doesn't belong or where it fits awkwardly. In making a point about the power of words vis-à-vis Matthew 12:36–37, the following illustration was used:

Even our superstitions reveal the power of words. An old superstition has it that when you sneeze your soul leaves your body, and unless you are promptly blessed, you are possessed by demons. When you sneeze, therefore, a word is spoken: "Gesundheit," the German word for health; "God bless you"; or, if you're from the South, "Scat!" Just saying the word has the power to save you from devils.

Is this illustration, however, about the power of words or the power of superstitions? The illustration is not irrelevant, just a bit awkward. A better tact would be to find out what a famous author regarded as the five or ten most powerful words in the English language.

In addition to appropriateness, two other factors influence relevance as well, timeliness and audience. Timeliness has to do with being contemporary. Make sure your passing anecdotal references are not dated. While recently thumbing through an old sermon about one of the kings of Israel, I noticed an analogy to his corrupt advisers that mentioned Jeb MacGruder and John Haldeman, two of Richard Nixon's advisers. The reference was timely in the early 1970's, but no longer. Statistics also must be timely. Don't use any statistics more than a couple of years old.

Keep in mind that the audience helps determine what is relevant. Select illustrative material to which the audience can relate. Don't use your farm stories in Brooklyn.

Question Two: Is It Transparent?

Is the illustration clear and understandable, needing no explanation? Consider the following quotation by the American essayist, John Jay Chapman, "A vision of truth which does not call upon us to get out of our armchair—why, this is the desideratum of mankind." Do you think your congregation will catch the relatively unfamiliar word "desideratum"? If you have to define it, the quotation is worthless. (Changing the word to "desire" is not objectionable, but let your conscience guide you).

Bluntly stated, if the illustration needs to be illustrated, it needs to be thrown away. Sweazey advises, "Do not use an illustration to illustrate an illustration—grace is like an electric relay which you can understand if you think of a man controlling the floodgates of a dam. If the first illustration is not clear by itself, it cannot be saved."[2]

Transparency is also achieved by choosing illustrations that force a single conclusion and avoid ambiguity. The following anecdote is told by Robert Schuller:

> Dr. Henry Poppen, who spent over forty years as a missionary to China, once shared with me his experience of going to a remote village, where presumably missionaries had never been. There he told the people about Jesus, how he was gentle and kind, and that he was able to forgive easily and loved even those who were unlovable.
>
> When Dr. Poppen finished telling them about Jesus, some of the men came to him and said, "We know Jesus! He has been here!"
>
> "No," said Dr. Poppen. "He lived and died in a country that is far away from here."
>
> "No, no," they replied. "He died here. Come, we'll show you his grave."
>
> They led him outside the city to a cemetery where only one American was buried. There on the tombstone was the name of a Christian medical doctor, who, all on his own, felt called by Jesus Christ to go there, live there, and die there. Now the people thought he was Jesus . . . [3]

Apart from its context, the story could either be about a saintly doctor who was Christlike or a dangerous cultist who advertized himself as Christ. Equivocal anecdotes, quotations, or statistics should be avoided unless they can be easily explained or are firmly grounded in the context of the sermon.

Question Three: Is It True?

This question does not have to do with whether the material is fiction or nonfiction, but whether it is true in fact and detail? Is the quotation accurately quoted and correctly attributed? Are the dates, names, and places mentioned in the anecdote correct?

Martyn Lloyd-Jones relates the following story about an illustration with mismanaged facts.

> I remember when I was a young medical man listening to a sermon in which there was a great illustration which the preacher unfolded at some considerable length. His point was, the folly of the sinner in not paying attention to the first warnings of his conscience and so on. This was illustrated very elaborately by the story of a woman whom he had buried the week before. She had had a cancer in one breast, but by the time she had gone to the doctor the secondary deposits had already spread to the spine and other parts of her body. It was now too late for a cure. What was the matter with this woman? "Well," said the preacher, "the tragedy of this woman was she did not pay attention to the first twinge of pain." To me, listening as a medical man, the whole thing was utterly ridiculous. The trouble with that sort of cancer is that it does not give you any pain until it has generally advanced to a considerable extent; it grows insidiously and quietly. The trouble with that poor woman was not that she had ignored pain, but probably had ignored a small lump which she may have felt. The great illustration was ruined as far as I was concerned because the man did not know his facts.[4]

Truthfulness also involves believability. Even if it is true, an unbelievable story will not ring true to an audience. William Sangster tells of going to a lavish wedding reception where the bride sat off in a corner of the reception hall largely ignored by all the guests. He used the illustration in an Advent sermon to show how Christ is often pushed to the side in our Christmas revelry. Even though true, the wedding story was so improbable that many in the congregation dismissed it as a homiletical fabrication.[5] Truth is stranger than fiction, but make sure your illustrations are not too strange.

The truthfulness of our illustrations—the way we handle the facts—is an issue with profound implications for an entire ministry. Credibility is at stake. If you mishandle an illustration, can you be trusted to correctly handle the word of truth (2 Timothy 2:15)? Can a person who is careless with the facts be counted on to be careful as a counselor, adviser or leader? Ask mercilessly of every illustration, Is it true?

Question Four: Is It Interesting?

What a person finds interesting depends a lot on personal taste. Some interest factors transcend subjective preference, however, and the preacher should be aware of these. Generally speaking, people are more interesting than things. Conflict, mystery, sex, death, and money interest most people. History is not all that interesting, which explains why the illustration cited in chapter 2 about Julius Caesar's adoption of Octavian lacked appeal. Topics like athletics, politics or feminism also will be interesting to a segment of the congregation.

A preacher can maintain interest by using a good variety of illustrative material. Illustrations must reach beyond the preacher's own interests and hobbies to include material of interest to others. Sometimes the speaker's own attitude and enthusiasm about the illustration sparks interest in people who would otherwise be disinterested. Also, the speaker can use numerous simple details of fact in anecdotes to help heighten interest.

Another method to create and maintain interest involves delivery. Webb Garrison makes the point that the preacher must enter into the illustration with emotional verve so that the congregation will also enter in emotionally. He cites a story told about John Whitefield.

Qualities

According to early Methodist tradition, Lord Chesterfield sometimes sat in Lady Huntingdon's pew when Whitefield was preaching. On one occasion the evangelist illustrated a point by describing a blind beggar's progress along a winding road. Soon the traveler was deserted by his little dog, and forced to tap his way along the side of a sheer cliff. Stumbling, he dropped his stick. He stopped to pick it up, leaned over the edge of the precipice, and began swaying. "Great God," cried Chesterfield, "he's gone!"[6]

High energy delivery, appropriate to the emotional tone of the illustration, always enhances interest.

Question Five: Is It Brief?

Illustrations that are long or involved tend to distract from the biblical text and muddle the sermon's structure and flow. MacPherson writes, "Brevity, according to the adage, is the soul of wit; it is certainly something which must ever characterize the preacher who would have the wit to save souls."[7]

Of course, exceptions exist. A story sermon or a one-point, "bull's eye" message, may rely on one long anecdote. In most expository preaching, however, a variety of points revolve on a single idea and all of them need one or more illustrations. All this must be communicated in twenty to thirty minutes. Therefore, time is crucial.

In some cases, a long anecdote might be ten minutes in the telling. If the total time for the sermon is twenty-five minutes, little time remains for explanation and application of the text, not to mention the sermon's introduction and the development of other points. Occasionally, an especially relevant anecdote may include in itself all the explanation and application of the text necessary. Such anecdotes are rare. Usually when time runs short, it is the anecdote that has consumed it. Writing out an anecdote, then editing it down to the essential details, is the best way to both economize time and maximize the anecdote's strengths.

Rambling anecdotes are usually unwritten, unrehearsed, and finally ineffective.

Question Six: Is It Tactful?

Tact, like common sense, is frequently talked about but is not all that common. Tact has been defined as a "quick and fine perception of the proper thing to say or do to avoid giving offense; sensitive skill in dealing with people."[8] Tact is a most precious asset in the pulpit, a natural outgrowth of a preacher's love for God and people.

Tactfulness in preaching does not mean we will never denounce sin with the prophetic power of an Amos or Isaiah. What it does mean is that we will choose illustrations that do not detract from the biblical message through inadvertent insensitivity. Illustrations that demean or belittle individuals or groups are not acceptable. Sweazey quips, "In the present state of society about the only ethnic groups that can safely be portrayed in pulpit illustrations are Sumerians and Hittites."[9]

Tact demands the elimination of all overtones of racism and sexism. Use sarcastic humor carefully. Profanity within quotations might be tactful, but be careful. (A Mark Twain quote comes to mind: "History is one damned thing after another.") Tact does not keep us from telling the truth pointedly; it keeps us from the insensitivity that demeans the truth.

The six questions outlined in this chapter become second nature to preachers who have educated their intuition to discern sound illustrations. Just any illustration will not do. The goal is to use those that are as relevant, transparent, true, interesting, brief, and tactful as possible. The next point to consider involves where we can find such material.

5

Sources

It's said that at the end of the rainbow lies a pot of gold. At the end of the Yellow Brick Road Dorothy discovered the Wizard. Multitudes believe that at Lourdes the cure can be found. "But where," plead thousands of preachers every week, "can I find the illustrations I need for Sunday's sermon?" Does finding the right illustration have to be as daunting as traveling through Oz or as mysterious as a Lourdes cure?

Part of the problem of locating illustrations is that many preachers are not quite sure what they are looking for. However, having identified four basic types of illustrations and six criteria of quality, we are ready to consider where to find good illustrations. Educating one's intuition for the sound illustration demands familiarity with two principal sources.

Simply put, the only sources of illustrations are what you have read and what you have experienced.[1] Your experience is everything you have heard, seen or done. Unquestionably, an educated person's reading extends his or her familiarity with the world beyond personal experience. Both are important as sources of illustrations.

ILLUSTRATING THE SERMON

In terms of reading, three specific illustration sources merit consideration: periodicals, books, and collections of illustrations.

PERIODICALS

Newspapers and magazines are loaded with contemporary anecdotes, quotations, and statistics. Sangster advises that preachers choose a newspaper carefully and scan it daily for ideas.[2] This is not as time consuming as many imagine. Once you know your way around in your favorite paper, you can read even its beefiest weekday editions in thirty minutes or less.

To illustrate the kind of treasures the paper yields, I scanned the *New York Times* for one week for illustrative material. It was the first week in January of a recent year. What follows is a week's worth of illustrations from the *Times*. Following each illustration I've made a notation referring it to a specific text and/or file.

Wednesday, January 1

A holiday editorial appeared entitled, "Perfectibility." In answer to the question of why we make New Year resolutions, the editorial states:

> We do it because a long time ago we read that man was a little lower than angels, and we believed it. The possibility of perfection is the most enduring of all illusions, and its pursuit the most enduring of all quests. . . . Perfection, of course, is not within: unflawed is unhuman. But perhaps we are, after all, perfectible. We can come close, we tell ourselves. Maybe next time. Maybe next year. Maybe this year.

(File under: Christian Life/Holiness; or Doctrine/Perfection; or Matthew 5:48.)

Sources

Wednesday, January 1

A review of the book *Anxiety*, by Donald W. Goodman, contained the following wonderful quote about anxiety by Søren Kierkegaard (from "The Concept of Dread").

> No Grand Inquisitor has in readiness such terrible tortures as has anxiety and no spy knows how to attack more artfully the man he suspects, choosing the instant when he is weakest, nor knows how to lay traps where he will be caught and ensnared, as anxiety knows how, and no sharp witted judge knows how to interrogate, to examine the accused, as anxiety does, which never lets him escape, neither by diversion nor by noise, neither at work nor at play, neither by day nor by night.

(File under: Christian Life/Anxiety; or Philippians 4:6.)

Thursday, January 2

A short article from the Associated Press reported that a rare 328-year-old book, missing from the Pennsylvania state library for over a hundred years had been returned. Surprised officials discovered the 1658 manuscript in a book drop bin! The story bears a resemblance to Josiah's rediscovery of the Torah.
(File under: 2 Kings 22.)

Saturday, January 4

A news report told how a county District Attorney in New York planned to travel around the state to rouse a protest to the governor's grant of clemency to a convicted murderer. The District Attorney's action is a perfect imitation of Satan who goes about accusing sinners who have already been pardoned by God.
(File under: Job 1:6 and Revelation 12:10; or Doctrine/Satan.)

Sunday, January 5

A New Year editorial by the Nobel prize-winning scholar Elie Wiesel of Boston University concluded with these sentences:

> Humankind needs peace more than ever, for it has, more than ever, been saturated with violence and war. Now the entire planet is in danger. But peace is not God's gift to His creatures. It is our gift—to each other.

Wiesel's comment is the exact opposite of Jesus' statement in John 14:27.

(File under: John 14:27; or Doctrine/Peace.)

Five pieces of material from the newspaper in one week are as much as can be hoped for. Zero in on editorials, reviews of all kinds, the columnists, comics, and human interest stories. The paper you read will yield similar results as you grow more sensitive to relevant material.

Magazines offer illustrative material similar to that found in newspapers. News magazines (like *Time* and *Newsweek*), and general interest periodicals (like *The Atlantic* and *The New Yorker*), are the best sources. The narrowly focused, special interest magazines that have proliferated in recent years are of less value. Avoid quoting or referring to sleazy, second-rate periodicals like those sold in grocery store checkout lanes. They have no credibility, and neither will you if you use them for anything but humor.

BOOKS

Reading books will yield anecdotes, quotes, and statistics comparable to those found in periodicals. Preachers must be readers, and most are. The fault of many, however, is that religious titles constitute the bulk of their reading. The diet must be balanced. The best illustrations usually come from secular fiction, history, and biography. A sure way to discover worthwhile books is to become an avid reader of book reviews. A person who regularly reads newspapers and magazines should not find it difficult to read an average of three book reviews a week.

Certain books merit special consideration: the Bible, the hymnal, and reference books that guide the reader to illustrations.

Sangster reminds us that the Bible, as an illustration source, is in a class by itself.[3] As has already been pointed out, however, biblical illiteracy in the pew should make the preacher cautious when using biblical anecdotes. It may be true that the audience's lack of familiarity with biblical stories guarantees their freshness, but a real danger lies in the discrepancy between the preacher's knowledge of the Bible and the congregation's. The preacher is likely to be very familiar with a biblical anecdote while the congregation's knowledge is sketchy or nonexistent. If the preacher fails to take the time to explain the story adequately, the congregation ends up more confused than ever. Biblical anecdotes should definitely be part of your repertoire of illustrations, but use them "with great patience and careful instruction" (2 Timothy 4:2).

Without a doubt, the Bible is a great source of quotations. One of the first rules of hermeneutics is to let Scripture interpret Scripture. The application of this is revealed in how freely preachers quote the Bible. Like other quotations, biblical quotes must not be too long. Without altering the essential meaning, a long scriptural quotation can be edited so that it comes to the point directly and forcefully.

The hymnal can be mined for illustrations in two ways.[4] A speaker may either quote the lyrics of hymns or give an anecdote based on the hymn or hymnwriter. Because they are familiar, hymn lyrics have an emotive appeal beyond their intellectual content. Beautiful hymns add elegance to the sermon. Speakers can glean anecdotes about hymns from companion volumes to hymnals and from books devoted exclusively to such anecdotes.[5]

Another class of books important to the search for

illustrations is that of research reference books.[6] These references works are available in libraries and include, among others, *Public Affairs Information Service, New York Times Index, The Annual Register of World Events, Facts on File,* and *Famous First Facts.* A good almanac is also a rich source of illustrative data. Suffice it to say that most preachers do not reap information and illustrations from the reference sections of libraries nearly as much as they could.

COLLECTIONS OF ILLUSTRATIONS

When it comes to published collections of illustrations, many homileticians have arrived at the same forthright view as Sangster: burn all such volumes "or send the paper to be repulped and put to better use."[7] Sangster's advice is understandable but too radical. The value of the illustrations depends on the categories in the collection.

Anecdotes simply do not lend themselves to collection and publication in books. This is not to say that it hasn't been attempted—it has been, frequently.[8] The results, however, are uniformly disappointing, so much so that not one such volume comes to mind to recommend or even discuss.

Quotations, on the other hand, like postage stamps and antiques, are eminently collectible. Many volumes of quotations are in print and every preacher should own a half dozen (or the equivalent in software). The most important consideration when buying a book of quotations is its indexes. Ideally there should be four: topic, author, source, and first line. The topical index is most important. A quotation that includes two topics should be indexed under both. Experienced speakers will tell you that a book of quotations arranged only by author is worthless.

The quality of quotation collections largely depends on the interest and wit of the compiler. For example, *The Viking Book of Aphorisms: A Personal Collection,* by W. H. Auden and Louis Kronenberger, tends to be rather intellectual, even esoteric. *Speaker's Handbook of Epigrams and Witticisms* by Herbert V. Prochnow, however, is provocative, yet light and humorous.[9] So many quotation books are available that everyone's tastes can be accommodated.[10] Generally speaking, collections put together by journalists, speakers, and literati are the best; those compiled by preachers and academics the worst.

As far as collections of other kinds of illustrations are concerned, statistics are perishable commodities, usually out of date before they come to press. Like strawberries, they can be preserved only by being frozen or canned—and that is exactly how they will sound when used. Live demonstration ideas are rarely compiled and published. The closest you can come might be the books of Sunday school and children's sermon "object lessons."[11] And, finally, style is a personal creation that cannot be borrowed.

Not only do illustrations come from everything a preacher reads, but also from his or her own life experiences. For those who discipline themselves to observe, life itself clarifies and amplifies the Word of God.

As I was writing this chapter I was preparing a sermon on the eighth chapter of Amos. "This is what the Sovereign Lord showed me: a basket of ripe fruit. 'What do you see, Amos?' he asked. 'A basket of ripe fruit,' I answered. Then the Lord said to me, 'The time is ripe for my people Israel; I will spare them no longer' " (Amos 8:1–2). As I worked on the sermon, this incident occurred:

> I was grocery shopping for fruit for a fruit salad. The store displayed cantaloupe in two different locations. The main display had the best looking melons at the regular price. Off to one side, however, was a cart full of melons that looked like they had been used for soccer practice. The bruised, overripe melons were priced for quick sale and I knew that if I bought one I would have to use it right away. Amos's point? God's warning, like ripe fruit, demands urgent attention.

This anecdote is actually an illustration of an illustration. It is not very profound, but in the pulpit it will help bring the Word to life and the truth home.

ILLUSTRATING THE SERMON

Many personal anecdotes occur, not years in advance of the sermon in which they can be used, but during the course of weekly preparation. I was preaching a series on financial stewardship based on 2 Corinthians 8–9, where Paul tells how the Macedonians gave generously in spite of their extreme poverty. He also compares their giving with that of the Corinthians.

In the middle of the series I spoke on the phone with a missionary society representative about some unrelated matter. We began talking about finances and he told me he was constantly amazed at the giving of one particular group. He is often flabbergasted, he said, by the amounts given by retired missionaries. Here are people who have given their careers to God. Their pensions are meager but in retirement they give beyond all expectations for the support of younger missionaries going to the fields where they have served. Jack said, "Sometimes, Mike, I sit at my desk and weep when I see what they are giving."

Here was a perfect illustration of Macedonian-style giving—contemporary, relevant, and moving. I did nothing to create it. It was just there to be observed and repeated.

Two specific factors help greatly in seizing personal experiences to use as illustrations. One is planning, the other prayer. The farther ahead you plan your preaching texts and topics, the better your chances of finding good illustrations. The preacher who is on the lookout for two months has much better odds of success than the one who frantically scrambles at the last minute.

Prayer is also important. Anyone who has ever preached knows that providence plays a big part in sermon preparation. It stands to reason that, other factors being equal, God is more concerned about the success of your sermon than you are. Pray for illustrations.

Do you have trouble finding illustrations? Do you read? Are you alive? Open your eyes! Let all of your reading and all of your experiences be open to your educated intuition for the sound illustration.

6

Storage

One of the laws of hydrostatics is that a body immersed in a fluid loses as much in weight as the weight of an equal volume of the liquid. The Greek scientist Archimedes thought of this while bathing at the public baths. He was so excited over his discovery that he ran home naked shouting, "Eureka! Eureka! I have found it!"

A preacher who can quickly recover good illustrations from his or her files knows something of Archimedes' elation. Lost illustrations are not just lost, they're nonexistent. Most preachers, therefore, are more than a little interested in how pertinent anecdotes, quotations, and statistics, once found, can be rediscovered when needed.

Preachers ought to recognize at the outset that storing and retrieving sermon ideas, notes, and illustrations is work that requires discipline, time, and effort. There are no quick, painless methods. Methods advertized as being effortless are phony. Gordon MacDonald has pointed out that any storage and retrieval system must be "simple, quickly usable, reflective of one's thinking and style, and up-to-date. Beyond that, *all it needs is regular attention*" (italics added). Regular attention to the filing system is the key to success.

ILLUSTRATING THE SERMON

Most preachers already use some sort of filing method and that leads to a bit of advice: use the system you already have. Unless your system is an unworkable disaster (chances are, it isn't), don't throw it away and start over. It is far more time consuming and difficult to start a new system than to refurbish and update what you have.

GENERAL GUIDELINES

Since filing systems are highly personalized items, it is difficult to prescribe rules for their use. Figure out what works for you and stick with it. Here are some general guidelines that may be helpful.

1. Beware of starting out with index cards. A few cards are easy to handle, but did you ever try to sort through five hundred 3 x 5 cards? Also keep in mind that almost all your illustrations will have to be transferred on to the card from the original source.

2. Most material is best filed by text or topic, requiring two sets of file folders, one for the books of the Bible and another alphabetized set for topics. Alphabetized files are fairly convenient to work with because they can easily be subdivided and expanded.

3. Avoid systems that require cross-filing. Keep it simple.

4. Don't write off published systems, especially if you are just getting started. However, be flexible and modify the system to fit your needs.

5. If it works, it's right. Even if no one else on the planet understands your system, if it works for you, it's a success.

COMPUTERIZED SYSTEMS

Computerized collections of sermon ideas and illustrations are available.[2] Should you buy one? Is the computer the answer to sorting and retrieving illustrations? These are difficult questions. There is little doubt that computers are a worthwhile addition to the church office, but it remains to be seen how valuable they are in the specialized and highly personal work of sermon preparation.

When considering computerized illustration files, you need to answer this question: Is your computer currently a tool or a toy? Is it an indispensable piece of equipment or a gizmo you like to play with? To find out, answer true or false to these four statements.

1. You have a keyboard and monitor at the desk where you work and prepare sermons.

2. You turn your computer on first thing in the morning and leave it on all day.

3. You constantly use the computer for long and short range scheduling, phone numbers, memos, letters, and the like.

4. You are proficient at keyboarding (typing).

If all of these statements are true, then your computer is a tool. If even one is false, chances are your computer is a toy. Until your machine becomes a tool, it is probably not wise to invest in computerized illustration files.

How good are computerized collections of illustrations? They are probably no better and no worse than the books of collected illustrations. If you often look for illustrations collected in books, then you will probably use computerized collections as well. If, on the other hand, you don't like what you find in books, it is unlikely you will appreciate illustrations from disks.

One advantage of computerized sources might be timeliness because computerized collections can be published faster than books. But keep in mind that illustrations won't sound any different in the pulpit if they come off a disk or a piece of paper. Also, regardless of where an illustration is stored, it will need to be transcribed or somehow incorporated into the notes that are carried to the pulpit.

The other dimension of computerized files is that you can make your own. You can store your own material in the computer instead of a filing cabinet. Before you choose this alternative, consider two factors: time and volume. (It takes time to type an anecdote, magazine article or review into the computer—more time than it takes to drop a piece of paper into a file folder. This is true regardless of who does the work, the preacher or the secretary. Remember, too, that computers are designed to handle large amounts of information. How many illustrations do you need to store in a year? Four hundred seems high, but to a computer, storing four hundred pieces of data hardly taps into its potential. Filing your illustrations in a computer might be akin to going after the mouse in the kitchen with an MX missile.

If you are comfortable and proficient with a computer and use one constantly, it may be the best storage system for you. If not, stick with the more traditional hard copy methods.

Whatever system you devise to store illustrations, remember that perfecting it is just as important as perfecting your intuition for good illustrations. Without an adequate storage system, your intuitive skill, no matter how finely tuned, is likely to be wasted.

7

Reviews

A few years ago the religion editor of the *Cleveland Press*, George Plagenz, developed a unique approach to his job. Every Monday he published a review of the worship service he attended the day before. The reviews, modeled on those for restaurants and movies, touched four elements: the service, music, sermon, and congregational friendliness. A perfect score was twelve stars, three for each category.[1]

If worship services can be reviewed like restaurants, then why not sermon illustrations? What follows are twenty-five examples of illustrations, along with reviews. All the illustrations have been given a title and identified by type. The sources are briefly noted along with a suggestion for filing. Stars have been awarded as follows:

> No star: poor, unusable
> One star: fair
> Two stars: good
> Three stars: very good
> Four stars: outstanding

The comments that follow each illustration explain the rating. Since subjective preferences obviously come into the evaluations, not all preachers will rate these illustrations the same. These are included to help you develop your intuition for sound illustrations by comparing your impressions with those given.

★★★ Lesson in Honesty (Contemporary Anecdote)

Letter received at the Brooklyn Botanic Garden from a youngster in the Bronx:

Dear Brooklyn Botanic Garden,
   I took a quarter out of the wishing well. So I feel so bad that I am returning your quarter back to you.
                                           Thank you,
                                           Chris

Letter sent by the president of the Brooklyn Botanic Garden:

Dear Chris:
   We are very glad to have your letter and the 25-cent piece enclosed with it. Clearly, you have learned how important it is to be an honest person.
   I hope that you will enjoy the book enclosed and that you will visit the garden again soon.
                                           Sincerely,
                                           Donald E. Moore
               Source: *New York Times*, 17 June 1987

Several qualities make this story compelling: it's true and simple, combining insights into honesty, guilt, confession, restitution, and grace. The only possible weakness is that no single topic stands out.

(File under: Honesty or Ephesians 4:28.)

★ A Gracious Priest (Historical Anecdote)

During World War I a small band of American soldiers knocked on the door of a Catholic Church in France seeking permission to bury their dead comrade in the church yard. The old parish priest asked them,

"Was your friend a member of the true faith?" The men replied, "He was a Christian, the member of a Baptist church in America." "I'm sorry," the priest replied, "the church yard is dedicated ground. Church law allows only for the burial of Catholics. However, if you'd like, you can bury your friend just outside the fence." The soldiers did so and returned the next day with some flowers to scatter on the grave. To their utter amazement, the grave that had been outside the church yard was now inside the fence. The men discovered that during the night the priest had uprooted several fence posts and rerouted the fence to include the Protestant soldier.

Source: Unknown, heard in a sermon.

This story may not be true. It lacks the specific details that usually mark a true account and resembles the type of anecdotes found in books of illustrations. The redeeming part of the story, however, is that it makes a Catholic priest a hero, turning the tables on the prejudices of a Protestant audience. Touché!

(File under: Grace.)

★ Clear Channels (Contemporary Anecdote)

Mr. Franklin D. Roosevelt introduced the fireside chats of the presidents of the United States to the people. In an unobstructed way, the president could speak to millions of people and sweep the nation by his will or his voice. On the contrary, the Voice of America, which propagandizes the satellite states of the Communist orbit, is often jammed by powerful stations within the borders of Russia itself. These two experiences illustrate what may happen to the Word of God. The channels may be clear so that the Word will have free course and be glorified, or the channels may be jammed by obstruction, hatred, and thwarting on the part of evil and perverse men. Only as the Word of God has free course in our hearts, in our homes, in our society will we have the prosperity of the Lord.

ILLUSTRATING THE SERMON

Source: *The Church in God,* by Harold J. Ockenga

The contrast between the fireside chats and the Voice of America was contemporary when first used in the 1950's. Now, however, the contrast is dated. As an historical anecdote, however, the analogy seems somewhat boring.
(File under: 1 Thessalonians 2:13.)

★★★ The Tree That Disappeared (Personal Anecdote)

In the fall of 1985, the biggest tree in our neighborhood—which was in our front yard—was irreparably damaged by Hurricane Gloria. Several days after the storm, a crew of workers took down the 65 foot tree in just two or three hours. Sometime later a large machine was brought in that reduced the stump to a pile of sawdust. Today you can't even tell if a tree was ever there.

Once in a while an illustration comes along that fits beautifully with a particular text. In this case the text is rather obscure, but the fit is perfect.
(File under: Amos 2:9. "I destroyed the Amorite before them, though he was tall as the cedars and strong as the oaks. I destroyed his fruit above and his roots below.")

★ Magnificent Faith (Quotation)

When one remembers the actual position of affairs, the confident faith of such passages is seen to have been little short of magnificent. To this Christian prophet, spokesman of a mere ripple upon a single wave of dissent in the broad ocean of paganism, history and experience find unity and meaning nowhere but in the person of a blameless Galilean peasant who had perished as a criminal in Jerusalem. So would such early Christian expectations appear to an outsider. He would be staggered by the extraordinary claims advanced on behalf of its God by this diminutive sect, perhaps more than staggered by the prophecy that imperial authority over the visible and invisible worlds lay ultimately in the hands of this deity, whose power was not limited to his own adherents.

Source: *Commentary on Revelation,* by James Moffatt

This quotation has a powerful stylistic flourish, but its sentence structure makes it difficult to follow. Perhaps one line could be quoted easily: "History and experience find unity and meaning nowhere but in the person of a blameless Galilean peasant who has perished as a criminal."

(File under: Revelation.)

★★★ A New Name (Contemporary Anecdote)

Notice to Applicants

(1) Every person has the right to adopt any name by which he or she wishes to be known simply by using that name consistently and without intent to defraud.

(2) A person's last name (surname) does not automatically change upon marriage, and neither party to the marriage must change his or her last name. Parties to a marriage need not have the same last name.

(3) One or both parties to a marriage may elect to change the surname by which he or she wishes to be known after the solemnization of the marriage by entering the new name in the appropriate space provided in the Affidavit Section of this application. Such entry shall consist of one of the following surnames:

    (i) the surname of the other spouse; or

    (ii) any former surname of either spouse; or

    (iii) a name combining into a single surname all or a segment of the premarriage surname or any former surname of each spouse; or

    (iv) a combination name separated by a hyphen, provided that each part of such combination surname is the premarriage surname, or any former surname, of each of the spouses.

(4) The use of this option will have the effect of providing a record of the change of name. The marriage certificate, containing the new name, if any, constitutes proof that the use of the new name, or the retention of the former name, is lawful.

(5) Neither the use of, nor the failure to use, this option of selecting a new surname by means of this application abrogates the right of each person to adopt a different name through usage at some future date.

(OPTIONAL—Enter new surname in Item 1B and/or Item 11C on front side of record.)

Source: Instructions on the back of New York State marriage licenses

Thank God we will not have to read through such rigmarole when God gives us a new name! Legalese has the power to make whimsy of even the most mundane business.

(File under: Revelation 2:17 and related texts dealing with new names.)

★★★ Keeping the Law (Quotation)

One of the most satisfying things about growing up Roman Catholic were the rules, which were not then, as we say now, flexible.

The only questions for us children were ones of degree: if you inadvertently ate baloney at lunch on Friday, would you go to hell if you were hit by a car during recess afterward? If you sucked on a cough drop in the car on the way to 9 o'clock mass, had you violated the communion fast requirements? Which was worse: to leave a piece of the Host stuck to the roof of your mouth all through breakfast, or to move it with your finger, in direct violation of what the nuns had told you about stuck Hosts?

Is it any wonder I became accustomed to the letter of the law? Rules were a relief. They were like basic tap-dance combinations: you could set them up any way you pleased, add the stray shuffle or heel and toe, but at least you didn't have to improvise everything.

Source: Columnist Anna Quindlen in *The New York Times*

Anyone who's ever lived with rules knows the feeling. The quote is humorously down to earth, but at the same time raises provocative points about legalism.

(File under: Law, Romans, Galatians.)

★★★ Day of Hate (Contemporary Anecdote)

CAIRO, Aug. 2—Iran, vowing to avenge the deaths of hundreds of Iranian pilgrims in a riot in Mecca, called today for the "uprooting" of the Saudi Arabian royal family, raising the specter of religious war in the already tense Persian Gulf region.

According to the official Islamic Republic News Agency, one million Iranians converged on the Parliament building in Teheran today, screaming "Revenge! Revenge!" in a rally marking what was officially described as "a day of hate."

Source: Newspaper

An organized, official day of hate? This offers Christian preachers a perfect example of corporate depravity and the exact opposite of longsuffering love for which Christianity stands.

(File under: Love, Sin, Ephesians 4:31.)

★★★ The Virgin Birth (Quotation)

To a twentieth-century mind the notion of a virgin birth is intrinsically and preposterously inconceivable. If a woman claims—such claims are made from time to time—to have become pregnant without sexual intercourse, no one believes her. For centuries millions of people never doubted that Mary had begotten Jesus without the participation of a husband or lover. Nor was such a belief limited to the simple and unlettered; the most profound and most erudite minds, the greatest artists and craftsmen, found no difficulty in accepting the Virgin Birth as an incontestable fact. . . .

Are we, then, to suppose that our forebears who believed implicitly in the Virgin Birth were gullible fools, whereas we, who would no more believe in such notions than we would that the world is flat, have put aside childish things and become mature? Is our scepticism one more manifestation of our having—in Bonhoeffer's unhappy phrase—come of age? It would be difficult to support such a proposition in the light of the almost inconceivable credulity of today's brain-washed public, who so readily believe absurdities in advertisements and in statistical and sociological prognostications before which an African witch-doctor would recoil in derision.

Source: *Jesus: The Man Who Lives*, by Malcolm Muggeridge

The quote is long and probably needs to be edited. The passing reference to Bonhoeffer would probably be lost on most audiences. Otherwise this is a powerful piece.
(File under: Virgin Birth, Matthew 1.)

★★★ Golden Rule Text (Contemporary Anecdote)

The happiest people are those who help others.

Is that true of the people you know? Psychologist Bernard Rimland, at the Institute for Child Behavior Research in San Diego, has just published a simple test.

Make a list of 10 persons whom you know the best. After each name write either H (for happy) or N (for unhappy). Then go down the list again, this time writing S (for selfish) or U (for unselfish) after each name. Rimland defines selfishness as "a stable tendency to devote one's time and resources to one's own interests and welfare—an unwillingness to inconvenience oneself for others." Once you have completed your list, draw a table . . . , count each category, and place the numbers in the appropriate cell.

When Rimland added up the cases of 1,988 people rated by 216 students in six college classes, he found that the happy/selfish cell was almost empty (only 78 of the cases), while 827 cases fell into the happy/unselfish cell. Paradox: Selfish people are by definition devoted to bringing themselves happiness. Judged by others, however, they seem to succeed less often than people who work at bringing happiness to others.

Conclusion: Do unto others as you would have them do unto you.

Source: Chris Cox in *Psychology Today*, December 1982

This "test" does nothing more than confirm the obvious, but it will fit in nicely the next time you preach on Matthew 7:12.

(File under: Matthew 7:12, The Golden Rule.)

★★ Carrying the Stone (Fictional Anecdote)

A story is told of Jesus and His disciples walking one day along a stony road. Jesus asked each of them to choose a stone to carry for Him. John, it is said, chose a large one while Peter chose the smallest. Jesus led them then to the top of a mountain and commanded that the stones be made bread. Each disciple, by this time tired and hungry, was allowed to eat the bread he held in his hand, but of course Peter's was not sufficient to satisfy his hunger. John gave him some of his.

Some time later Jesus again asked the disciples to pick up a stone to carry. This time Peter chose the largest of all. Taking them to a river, Jesus told them to cast the stones into the water. They did so, but looked at one another in bewilderment.

"For whom," asked Jesus, "did you carry the stone?"

Source: *These Strange Ashes*, by Elisabeth Elliot

The story speaks for itself, but deciding exactly what it illustrates may be more difficult than it first appears. Is it about obedience, sacrifice, selfishness, commitment . . . ? The danger of general-purpose stories like this one is that they are often thrown into the sermon for general purposes, without careful thought. Before using, decide specifically on the idea to be illustrated.

(File under: Obedience.)

★★ What Do You Believe In? (Fictional Anecdote)

At the very end of the motion picture *Sleeper*, Woody Allen and Diane Keaton discuss their beliefs. She says, "You don't believe in science and you also don't believe political systems work and you don't believe in God, huh? So then, what do you believe in?" Woody Allen replies, "Sex and death, two things that come once in my lifetime."

Source: The motion picture *Sleeper*

If you think Mr. Allen's reply is too risky for your congregation, tact might require leaving this one in the file. Otherwise, it's a good example of the views of a lot of nonreligious people.

(File under: Faith, Belief, 2 Timothy 1:12.)

★★★★ Who Gives What (Statistic)

The Rockefeller Brothers Fund conducted a study [in a recent year] in order to determine a profile of charitable givers in America. Over 1100 adults were interviewed. Researchers discovered that on the average, Americans give about 2.4 percent of their income to charity. Religious organizations get 72 percent of all the money contributed. Protestants said they contributed about 2.9 percent of household income while Catholics gave 1.6 percent. Individuals under 35 tended to be less generous than others. Contributions to charity from living individuals in 1984 amounted to $61.5 billion.

Source: Newspaper

Such statistics quickly become dated. In their time, however, these numbers were informative, relevant, easy to understand, and impeccably credentialed.

(File under: Giving, Finances, 2 Corinthians 8–9.)

★★★★ I Found This Bible (Personal Anecdote)

I always empty the church's mail box near the big wastebasket at the Post Office. Probably ninety percent of what we get is religious junk mail. Not so, however, with a parcel that recently arrived. It contained an old, green paperback *Living New Testament*. There's a name on the inside cover:

Danette Hill
Calvary Baptist Church
Ossining, NY

A note came with the Bible. Here it is:

Dear Danette:

At Word of Life Island camp in 1975, I heard the Good News and I became a follower of Christ. On one of the weekly walks around the island, I found this Bible. I picked it up and brushed it off. Since it was a readable edition for a 14 year old, I read it through faithfully during the next 6 months. It wasn't until I was at college with my many other editions of the Bible that my ex-boyfriend said I should return it. I'd never thought of it before. So now, if you still exist, I hope this Bible reaches you. Thanks for the loan—it started me off.

Sincerely in Christ,
Lynn Woodward
West Hurley, NY

Engaging true stories speak for themselves.
(File under: Bible, Isaiah 55:11.)

ILLUSTRATING THE SERMON

★★★★ Learning to Say Thanks (Personal Anecdote)

At first glance this flat command to be thankful would seem to take the joy, spontaneity, and genuineness out of our thankfulness. We could end up being thankful because we're supposed to be rather than because we really are. But further reflection on this command reveals both its wisdom and its appropriateness. This was brought home to me while trick-or-treating with my kids a few years ago. Before hitting the street, I lectured Spiderman and Bozo that they were supposed to say thank-you when given a treat. My lecture was accompanied with appropriate threats that if their gratitude wasn't verbally expressed they would be on their way home sooner than they expected. I listened carefully at the first few houses and, as feared, their thank-you's were inaudible. After each failure I reviewed the fact that only barbarians accept something without saying thank-you and since we weren't barbarians we had better start saying thank-you, etc.

Finally they began to catch on—reluctantly at first, but gaining in enthusiasm until at the end of the evening they were genuinely expressing their appreciation.

How like the children we all are! God knows we must be told to be thankful in order to get us started. After we get started, based on the command, we discover the joy of spontaneous and genuine thanksgiving. Without the command we would not have started at all.

True stories are always best. This one beautifully addresses the paradox between spontaneous thanksgiving and the command to be thankful found frequently in Scripture.

(File under: Thanksgiving, 1 Thessalonians 5:18.)

★★★ Come Unto Me (Quotation)

"Come unto me," I hear, and the words move me more than I can say. Why should they move me? Why shouldn't they leave me cold or bore me to death?

In an elegant house on Long Island one summer Sunday, down a long table cluttered with silver and crystal and the faces and hands of strangers, my hostess suddenly directs a question at me. She is deaf and speaks in the ringing accents of the deaf, and at the sound of her question all other conversation stops, and every face turns to hear my answer. "I understand that you are planning to enter the ministry," she says. "Is this your own idea, or have you been poorly advised?"

I had no answer, and even if I'd had one, it wouldn't have been shoutable, and even if I'd shouted it, she couldn't have heard it, so the question was never answered and thus rings still unanswered in my head. How did I ever get involved in this business to begin with? By what implausible train of circumstances do I find myself standing here now? Why should the words of Jesus move me more than I can say?—Come unto me.

Source: *The Alphabet of Grace*, by Frederick Buechner

Specifically applying to Matthew 11:28, with a dash of humor, Buechner evokes the feeling of the faith needed to respond to Christ's invitation.

(File under: Matthew 11:28, Discipleship.)

★★★★ Love (Quotation)

The love for equals is a human thing—of friend for friend, brother for brother. It is to love what is loving and lovely. The world smiles.

The love for the less fortunate is a beautiful thing— the love for those who suffer, for those who are poor, the sick, the failures, the unlovely. This is compassion, and it touches the heart of the world.

The love for the more fortunate is a rare thing—to love those who succeed where we fail, to rejoice without envy with those who rejoice, the love of the poor for the rich, of the black man for the white man. The world is always bewildered by its saints.

ILLUSTRATING THE SERMON

And then there is the love for the enemy—love for
the one who does not love you but mocks, threatens,
and inflicts pain. The tortured's love for the torturer.
This is God's love. It conquers the world.

Source: *The Magnificent Defeat*, by Frederick Buechner

Style and substance combine to a crescendo in this
highly quotable passage.
(File under: Love, 1 Corinthians 13.)

(No stars) Arrival (Contemporary Anecdote)

There are all sorts of ways to know when you have
really "arrived." There are the usual indications, such
as title, business success, and financial achievements,
but there are other hints as well.

For example, when your children grow old enough
to seek your advice, you have "arrived." You also have
made it when you have lived in the same house long
enough to make the last mortgage payment. But there
are other signs too.

Recently we were enjoying dinner in a nice restaurant with a younger couple. The younger woman
ordered decaffeinated coffee. The rest of us ordered
regular coffee. When the waiter arrived, guess who got
the Sanka? The same waiter also assumed that the bill
was mine too. I accepted both as a token of "arrival."

Perhaps you have noticed other symbols. People
your own age begin to call you "sir" or "ma'am."
Policemen will look younger, and schoolteachers no
longer will seem to be eighty-five. And if you really are
in the age of arrival, your secretary will be younger than
your daughter.

At first all this is a shock, but all that it actually
means is that you have finally "arrived."

I'll bet you younger folks can't wait!

Source: *Illustrations Without Sermons* (a book of illustrations), by Bill Lufburrow

One speaker cannot use another speaker's first person stories with any degree of sense. You cannot put yourself in the author's place in the restaurant.

The difference between the other personal anecdotes in this chapter and this one is that the others are included simply as examples of illustrations while this one was published as an illustration for others to use. The point of including this story as an example of the unusable is simply to show the inherent weakness and insurmountable subjectivity of published personal anecdotes.

(File under: the desk.)

★★ Talk Show Reconciliation (Contemporary Anecdote)

Some time ago I was driving home from Bellevue, Washington, after a week of meetings. It was late on a Friday night. I had a drive of several hours ahead of me and I was weary. I turned on the radio and began to listen to a talk program as I drove down Interstate 5. After awhile I was about to turn to another station when a new voice, that of a young woman, caught my attention.

Her story began some eight years earlier when she met and fell in love with a fellow who was all she had desired in a man. The story has its rough edges, however; it is a story of our time. The man was married, but in the process of divorce. They decided to live together before the divorce decree was final.

One day the fellow's mother called and fussed at the woman for breaking up the marriage of her son. Actually, the couple had not met until the marriage was already in the divorce process. But as a consequence of her anger, the fellow's mother and the young woman never met.

Weeks passed. The divorce was final. The wedding date was set. Then the young man died in an automobile accident. Now the young woman was alone—and pregnant. She decided to move back to where her parents lived so she would have family near as her child was born.

The baby, a boy, became the center of her life. As he grew she lavished her love upon him, and through him remembered her warm love for the boy's father. Then her parents died and the woman was again alone in the world—just she and her child.

Then she thought, "I'm really not alone. The boy has a grandmother, even though she does not know about him." So she moved back to the city where she had met her fellow and she got a job at the same place the grandmother worked. They became friends on the job. And then they went to a company picnic where they shared a blanket and a basket and enjoyed the little boy together.

Now she was on the phone asking for advice from a nationally aired radio talk program host. "How am I going to tell her that the darling little boy she made so much over is really her grandson?"

The program host told her she could not just say, "By the way, that's your grandson." She would have to build up to it and would have to be prepared for rejection. The host suggested that the young woman call the older lady that night and invite her to dinner at her home for one day next week.

"Tell her that this will be the most important dinner of her life. Then, on the day of the dinner, tell her again how important this is. Tell her to be prepared for a shock."

She said, "All right. I'll do it. I'll call her tonight."

Then the host said, "After the dinner, call again so we can know what happened."

At that point I had this sinking feeling I would never know how this story came out. I had been so caught up in the story and its basic humanity that I found it was all I could think about. I turned down the sound and I began to pray for this young woman, for her son, and her son's grandmother. I prayed that God would direct the phone call, the meeting, and the reconciliation between these three needy people.

I did not know them. But they were each in need of the gracious action of God. And he is free and he is able to work his pleasure. I prayed that he would bring into their lives a sense of shelter in the shadow of his care.

Sometime later on the drive, I was nearly to the end of the reception area for this Seattle station. I was about to turn to another station when I heard the voice of the young woman again. I couldn't believe it! Programs like this do not let a person call back during the same broadcast. Yet there she was!

I could hardly hear the station now. I began slowing down. I was nearly ready to turn around and head back to Seattle to hear what she had to say.

"You won't believe this," she said. "I called, as you said I should. I told her I wished to invite her to my home for a very important dinner next week. As I said this, she screamed out, 'It was you! It is my grandson!' "

It turns out that the grandmother was listening to the same program. She had not recognized the voice of the young woman, for she had not any idea that her son might have fathered a child. As she listened to the program she kept thinking two things: "Whoever she calls will be the happiest woman in the world tonight. And I just wish it were I."

And it was she!

The host of the program was stunned. She gasped, "Hallelujah!" Then she was overcome. She went to an unscheduled commercial break. Then, with a voice heavy with emotion, she said, "I don't think anything like this has ever happened on a radio talk program. This is unbelievable!"

And it was.

God had moved.

God had stepped into a situation of hurting people and had done a wonder. I say this, not knowing if any of the principals know the Lord. But I know the Lord, and I know the incident was a work of his grace. This story demanded of me the praise that is due his name.

Source: *A Shelter in the Fury,* by Ronald B. Allen

In both his book and in a sermon I heard him preach, Ronald Allen used this fascinating story to illustrate the

difference between praise and thanksgiving as he understands it. The connection of these themes to this anecdote is
not transparent, to say the least. An illustration must bear an
intrinsic relationship to the point it illustrates. Otherwise it is
simply not relevant, no matter how engaging.

This particular anecdote, while rather involved, could
provide a solid illustration of providence, common grace, or
reconciliation.

(File under: Reconciliation, Providence.)

★★★★ The Dunmow Flitch (Historical Anecdote)

In England, connubial contentment could win the
Dunmow Flitch—a side, or flitch, of bacon awarded to
any couple who could come to Dunmow in Essex after a
year of marriage and truthfully swear that they never
quarreled and did not regret the marriage and would do
it over again if given the chance.

Source: *A Distant Mirror*, by Barbara Tuchman

Tuchman fails to mention if there is record of the flitch
ever being won!
(File under: Weddings, Marriage, Ephesians 5.)

★★★★ God Is Coming (Historical Anecdote)

One night, after midnight, he [Kamante, the Kenyan
cook] suddenly walked into my bedroom with a hurri-
cane-lamp in his hand, silent, as if on duty. It must have
been only a short time after he came into my house, for
he was very small; he stood by my bedside like a dark
bat that had strayed into the room, with very big
spreading ears, or like a small African Will-o'-the-wisp,
with his lamp in his hand. He spoke to me very
solemnly. "Msabu," he said, "I think you had better get
up." I sat up in bed bewildered; I thought that if
anything serious had happened, it would have been
Farah who would have come to fetch me, but when I
told Kamante to go away again, he did not move.
"Msabu," he said again, "I think that you had better get

up. I think that God is coming." When I heard this, I did get up, and asked why he thought so. He gravely led me into the dining-room which looked West, toward the hills. From the door-windows I now saw a strange phenomenon. There was a big grass-fire going on, out in the hills, and the grass burning all the way from the hill-top to the plain; when seen from the house it was nearly a vertical line. It did indeed look as if some gigantic figure was moving and coming toward us. I stood for some time and looked at it, with Kamante watching by my side, then I began to explain the thing to him. I meant to quiet him for I thought that he had been terribly frightened. But the explanation did not seem to make much impression on him one way or the other; he clearly took his mission to have been fulfilled when he had called me. "Well yes," he said, "it may be so. But I thought that you had better get up in case it was God coming."

Source: *Out of Africa*, by Isak Dinesen

The beauty of this account, which would be used as a quotation, lies in its evocation of mystery and expectation.

(File under: Second Coming of Christ, Revelation 22:20 and parallels.)

★ A Divorce Statistic (Statistic)

Couples who lived together before marrying have nearly an 80 percent higher divorce rate than those who did not and they seem to have less regard for the institution, according to a study of Swedish women by the National Bureau of Economic Research in Cambridge, Mass.

Source: *The New York Times*, 8 December 1987

At first glance, the findings of the study seem to confirm our suspicions about unmarried couples who live together. But wait, the study was done in 1981 and involved Swedish women, not Americans. Further, 12 percent of Swedish couples cohabit before marriage compared to only 4 percent of American couples. No conscientious speaker could feel as comfortable with this data as with the "Who Gives What" statistic cited earlier.

(File under: Marriage, Divorce, Ephesians 5.)

The following is a story told by comedian Emo Philips:

★★★★ Baptist on the Bridge (Quotation)

Once I was in San Francisco, walking across the Golden Gate Bridge, when I saw this guy on the bridge about to jump. I thought I'd try to stall him, detain him, long enough for me to put the film in. I said, "Don't jump."

He turned his head. You've heard of the Elephant Man? He had a head like the head of a horse. My heart went out to him. I said, "Why the long face?"

He said, "All my life people have called me mean names, cruel names like 'Flicka' . . . 'Chess Piece' . . . 'Trigger' . . . 'Silver' . . .' "

I said, "Don't worry about it, Ed."

He said, "Nobody loves me."

I said, "God loves you."

"How do you know there's a God?"

I said, "Of course there's a God. Do you think that billions of years ago, a bunch of molecules floating around at random without rhyme or reason could someday have had the sense of humor to make you look like that?"

He said, "I guess you're right." And a tear came to his eye.

I said, "Are you a Christian or a Jew or a Hindu or what?"

He said, "A Christian."

I said, "Small world! Me too. Protestant or Catholic or Geek Orthodox?"

He said, "Protestant."

I said, "Me too! What franchise?"

He said, "Baptist."

I said, "Me too! Northern Baptist or Southern Baptist?"

He said, "Northern Baptist."

I said, "Me too! Northern Conservative Baptist or Northern Liberal Baptist?"

He said, "Northern Conservative Baptist."

I said, "Me too! Northern Conservative Fundamentalist Baptist or Northern Conservative Reformed Baptist?"

He said, "Northern Conservative Fundamentalist Baptist."

I said, "Me too! Northern Conservative Fundamentalist Baptist Great Lakes Region or Northern Conservative Fundamentalist Baptist Eastern Region?"

He said, "Northern Conservative Fundamentalist Baptist Great Lakes Region."

I said, "Me too! Northern Conservative Fundamentalist Baptist Great Lakes Region Council of 1879 or Northern Conservative Fundamentalist Baptist Great Lakes Region Council of 1912?"

He said, "Northern Conservative Fundamentalist Baptist Great Lakes Region Council of 1912."

I screamed, "DIE HERETIC!" And I pushed him over.

Source: Routine by comedian Emo Philips,
transcribed from video

The full force of this piece's humor is felt much more in hearing than reading it. Humorous material usually requires rehearsal out loud. In this case, the speech rate should increase toward the climax.

(File under: Schisms, 1 Corinthians 1.)

★★★★ The Bum at the Door (Personal Anecdote)

Our church is located in a rather rundown section of town. Panhandlers are fairly common and occasionally press their requests at my office door. Sometimes I can help, but common sense prohibits the distribution of cash on demand.

One Sunday I arrived at the office early to prepare for the day's services. The doorbuzzer rang, and I could see a stranger, obviously a bum, through the glass. I knew what he wanted, but for some reason I didn't want to deal with it that morning. I froze in the hallway, motionless, hoping he would think no one was in and go away. He was persistent. Finally my conscience got to me, and I opened the door.

The man's eyes were bloodshot, and he reeked of alcohol. Before I could say anything, he thrust a twenty-dollar bill into my hand, muttered something about my giving this to someone who needed it worse than he did, and staggered away down the sidewalk.

The sermon text for that day, chosen weeks in advance, was the saying of Jesus: "Here I am! I stand at the door and knock. If anyone hears my voice and opens the door, I will come in" (Rev. 3:20).

Stories of reversed charity are fairly common, but this one has the added dimension of its relevance to the text chosen for the day it happened.

(File under: God's providence; Revelation 3:20.)

★★★★ A Great Liar (Contemporary Anecdote)

Dear Diary,

Another grandchild story, if you can bear it.

Grandmother takes her two grandchildren out to lunch and they misbehave. On the way home one of them, a 7-year-old girl, asks, "Will you tell Mother how we acted?"

Self-righteous grandmother answers, "No, but if she should ask, I can't lie."

Whereupon, the boy said, "What do you mean you can't lie? I'm only 5 years old, and I can lie great!"

Source: Newspaper

Everybody can bear another grandchild story!
(File under: Truth, the Ninth Commandment.)

Conclusion

Self-Study Steps

Intuition has been defined as instantaneous apprehension. The development of intuition, however, is anything but instantaneous. A preacher must work hard and be disciplined in order to develop an intuition for illustrating sermons.

One practical method of educating one's intuition for the sound illustration is self-study. A few hours of research can yield invaluable insights into one's proficiency with illustrations. I offer the following plan as one possible approach to analyzing sermons in light of their illustrations.

SELF-STUDY STEPS

Step 1: Gather the outlines or manuscripts of ten or fifteen sermons you have recently preached. Pick a cross section, not just those you thought were good.

Step 2: On a piece of paper with four headings (one for each type of illustration—not to include style), list under the proper heading all of the illustrations you can find in your notes.

Step 3: Analyze the results. Look for frequency. Anecdotes should predominate, followed by quotations, statistics, and live demonstrations. Are are types over- or under-used?

Step 4: Since anecdotes are most important, study them separately. On another sheet of paper subdivide your list into the varieties of anecdotes: biblical, historical, personal, contemporary, and fictional. Again, check frequency.

Step 5: Go back to chapter 4 and ask all six questions of each of the illustrations, especially the anecdotes. Is each relevant, transparent, true, interesting, brief, and tactful? If in doubt, ask someone's opinion, especially regarding transparency and tactfulness.

Step 6: Try to recall where you got the listed illustrations. List your sources. How much variety is there? Are you relying heavily on some sources while ignoring others? Can you turn to your files and find the sources easily?

Step 7: Evaluate your style. Listening to tapes of your preaching is time-consuming, but it may be the best way to discover how effectively you are using the language. In addition, in the sermon notes, pay special attention to how you have worded propositions, main points, and the title. Again, get the input of trusted advisers.

If you are not satisfied with your sermon illustrations, work to correct the deficiencies. Repeat the seven-step study after eighteen or twenty-four months and compare your results with the first study. You should be making progress. If not, consider enrolling in a continuing education course in preaching.

As long as preaching is part of your work, the need for sermon illustrations will not go away. The need will not be met by someone or something external, but by growing, inner intuitive acuity. Read, observe, think, study, pray— learn the sound of the sound illustration.

Notes

Introduction

1. W. E. Sangster, *The Craft of Sermon Illustration* (London: Epworth, 1954), 49.

2. Ian MacPherson, *The Art of Illustrating Sermons* (Nashville: Abingdon, 1964), 8.

Chapter One

1. George E. Sweazey, *Preaching the Good News* (Englewood Cliffs, N.J.: Prentice-Hall, 1976), 193.

2. An example is Clyde E. Fant, *Preaching for Today*, rev. ed. (San Francisco: Harper & Row, 1975).

3. Fred B. Craddock, *Preaching* (Nashville: Abingdon, 1985), 204.

4. Interactions with Craddock's views on style and stories are included in the discussions of those topics that follow.

5. Ian MacPherson, *The Art of Illustrating Sermons* (1964; reprint, Grand Rapids: Baker, 1976), 12.

6. C. H. Spurgeon, *Flashes of Thought* (London: Passmore & Alabaster, 1874), 218.

7. Louis Paul Lehman, *Put a Door on It! The How and Why of Sermon Illustration* (Grand Rapids: Kregel, 1975).

8. Spurgeon, *Flashes of Thought*, 218.

9. Haddon W. Robinson, *Biblical Preaching: The Development and Delivery of Expository Messages* (Grand Rapids: Baker, 1980), 149.

10. J. I. Packer, *Knowing God* (Downers Grove, Ill.: InterVarsity Press, 1973), 67.

11. H. A. Ironsides, *Studies in Book One of the Psalms* (New York: Loizeaux Brothers, 1952), 6.

12. Rebecca Manley Pippert, *Out of the Salt Shaker* (Downers Grove, Ill.: InterVarsity Press, 1979), 177–78.

Chapter Two

1. W. E. Sangster, *The Craft of Sermon Illustration* (London: Epworth, 1954), 4.

2. Ibid., 43.

3. John R. W. Stott, *Between Two Worlds* (Grand Rapids: Eerdmans, 1982), 243.

4. Harold J. Ockenga, *The Church in God* (Westwood, N.J.: Revell, 1956), 256–57.

5. Raymond Brown, *Christ Above All: The Message of Hebrews* (Downers Grove, Ill.: InterVarsity Press, 1982), 67.

6. See Cecil B. Murphey, "Personal Experience Adds Punch," *Christianity Today* (25 May 1979): 36–37.

7. For a helpful overview of the sermon as story movement, see Clyde E. Fant, *Preaching for Today*, rev. ed. (San Francisco: Harper & Row, 1975), 191ff.

8. Fred B. Craddock, *Preaching* (Nashville: Abingdon, 1985), 204.

9. George E. Sweazey, *Preaching the Good News* (Englewood Cliffs, N.J.: Prentice-Hall, 1976), 195.

10. Charles Rice, "The Preacher as Storyteller," *Union Seminary Quarterly Review* (Spring 1976): 176.

11. Recommended titles are William R. White, *Speaking in Stories: Resources for Christian Storytellers* (Minneapolis: Augsburg, 1982), and Augusta Baker and Ellin Greene, *Storytelling: Art and Technique* (New York: R. R. Bowker, 1977).

Notes

12. Alan Monroe and Douglas Ehninger, *Principles and Types of Speech*, 6th ed. (New York: Scott Foresman, 1967), 166–69. More recent calculations of this illustration fix the appearance of reptiles on Christmas Eve. The variable is the postulated age of the earth.

13. Lyle E. Schaller, *It's a Different World* (Nashville: Abingdon, 1987), 84.

Chapter Three

1. Russell Baker, "Dry as Dust," *The New York Times* (2 June 1987).

2. Fred B. Craddock, *Preaching* (Nashville: Abingdon, 1985), 196.

3. Haddon W. Robinson, *Biblical Preaching: The Development and Delivery of Expository Messages* (Grand Rapids: Baker, 1980), 177.

4. William Strunk, Jr., and E. B. White, *The Elements of Style* (New York: Macmillan, 1959), 52.

5. George E. Sweazey, *Preaching the Good News* (Englewood Cliffs, N.J.: Prentice-Hall, 1976), 125–46.

6. Anna Quindlen, "Life in the 30's," *The New York Times* (14 July 1988).

7. Lance Morrow, "The Morals of Gossip," Essay, *Time* (26 October 1981): 97.

8. Robinson, *Biblical Preaching*, 189.

9. Sweazey, *Preaching the Good News*, 127.

10. W. Robertson Nicoll, "An Appreciation," in Alexander Maclaren, *Expositions of Holy Scripture: John, Jude, and Revelation* (N.p.: S. S. Scranton, n.d.).

Chapter Four

1. J. B. Phillips, *Ring of Truth* (New York: Macmillan, 1967), 118–19.

2. George E. Sweazey, *Preaching the Good News* (Englewood Cliffs, N.J.: Prentice-Hall, 1976), 196.

3. Robert H. Schuller, *Reach Out for New Life* (New York: Bantam, 1979), 84.

4. D. Martyn Lloyd-Jones, *Preaching and Preachers* (Grand Rapids: Zondervan, 1971), 234.

5. W. E. Sangster, *The Craft of Sermon Illustration* (London: Epworth, 1954), 116–17.

6. Webb B. Garrison, *The Preacher and His Audience* (Westwood, N.J.: Revell, 1954), 190.

7. Ian MacPherson, *The Art of Illustrating Sermons* (Nashville: Abingdon, 1964), 23.

8. *Webster's Twentieth Century Dictionary*, Unabridged, 2d ed., S.V. "tact."

9. Sweazey, *Preaching the Good News*, 199.

Chapter Five

1. It might be argued that the imagination constitutes a third primary source of illustrations. However, the imagination is built largely on one's reading and experience. For a discussion of the imagination in preaching, see Faris D. Whitesell, *Power in Expository Preaching* (Westwood, N.J.: Revell, 1963), 103–17.

2. W. E. Sangster, *The Craft of Sermon Illustration* (London: Epworth, 1954), 61f.

3. Ibid., 53f.

4. See Alton L. Gansky, "Using the Hymnal for Illustrations," *Your Church* (Jan.-Feb. 1986): 18.

5. For example, see Kenneth W. Osbeck, *One Hundred One Hymn Stories* (Grand Rapids: Kregel, 1982) and *One Hundred One More Hymn Stories* (Grand Rapids: Kregel, 1985).

6. Cyril J. Barber, "How to Find Those Elusive Illustrations," *Christianity Today* (30 January 1976): 24. Also see his *Minister's Library* (Grand Rapids: Baker, 1974).

Notes

7. Sangster, *The Craft of Sermon Illustration*, 46.

8. A recent example is Bill Lufburrow, *Illustrations Without Sermons* (Nashville: Abingdon, 1985).

9. Prochnow's book (1955; reprint, Grand Rapids: Baker, 1965) has a delightful introductory essay on the history and use of epigrams.

10. A recent edition of *Books in Print* lists more than two hundred titles of books of quotations. Review several volumes at a public library before deciding to buy.

11. See the outstanding volume *Gospel-Telling: The Art and Theology of Children's Sermons* by Richard Coleman (Grand Rapids: Eerdmans, 1982).

Chapter Six

1. Gordon MacDonald, "Storing and Retrieving Sermon Material," *Leadership* (Summer 1987): 61–62.

2. For example, "The Illusaurus," produced by The Computer Assistant in Arlington, Texas.

Chapter Seven

1. Reported in *The Wall Street Journal* (12 June 1978).